REGULAR

*The Saga of a Regular Guy
from an Extraordinary Place*

REG CHRISTENSEN

Dear Tim,

*I hope you enjoy this
account of a time and place
far away.*

Sincerely,

Reg Christensen

ISBN: 1499799160
ISBN 13: 9781499799163

Acknowledgments

Thank you to Ann Cue and Carol Christensen
for compiling and formatting the photo section.

Thank you to my professional editor and publisher
who always do so well with preparing my words in presentable format.

Thank you to my family and my many friends
who have encouraged this project and reviewed the manuscript.
And more than that—thank you for being my eternal family
and friends, for that is what remains and matters
after this book is long forgotten.

Table of Contents

———⚬❈⚬———

One a Comin' and One a Goin'

"Well, Boots, you have one a comin' and one a goin'!"

The one speaking was old Doc Madsen. Boots was my dad. The "one a comin'" was me being born on September 1, 1951, in Mt. Pleasant, Utah, just six miles south of my hometown of Fairview. The "one a goin'" was my grandpa, Rich Pete, who died August 31, 1951—just twelve hours before I was born. Doc Madsen attended to both Grandpa and me.

My name is Reg Christensen—not "Redge," "Reggie," nor "Reginald." I was named after Reg Garff, who was my father's boss when he worked in the insurance industry. Reg was a gruff old guy—or at least pretended to be. One morning after he had spent the night at our home, he caught his pants on a nail as he descended the stairs. He turned to my older brother, who was following him, and said, "Young man, you go get a hammer and pound that nail in or I will pound you." I think he was kidding, but I took no chances. As I was his namesake, he favored me from among my siblings, and he often brought me a bag of candy when he came to visit. I had learned that I was small enough to squeeze between the stair treads into an unfinished area of our basement —as no one else in our family could do—and enjoy my treat by myself.

I like my rather unique name, but I do not like the many variations of it that people often use (Although there are occasional advantages— when a telemarketer calls and asks, "Is Reginald there?" I can honestly say that he is not). In an unusually bold move after my high school English teacher had mispronounced my name as "Redge," I told her after class, "I will write it on the board, and you pronounce it." I then proceeded to write "Keg," "Leg," "Peg," and "Reg." She gave the usual excuse: "Well, I assumed it was short for Reginald." I assured her that it was not. I think she got it right from then on. My wife helps people by saying, "It is pronounced like Greg only without the *G* on the front." My daughter's way is to say, "It is 'Reg' as in 'Regular.' Remember that he is just a regular guy." In fact, "Regular" became an occasional nickname for me among my daughter and her friends.

I have always considered myself to be a regular guy from a regular place, but more recently, I have come to realize that I am a regular guy from an *extraordinary* place. Fairview has such a rich and unique culture and a diverse and special populace. I lived a charmed childhood. My purpose in writing this memoir is to share my joy and appreciation with others. I hope my descendants will get to know me better and enjoy learning of my life and the lives of loved ones. I hope my friends will sense my appreciation for them for the great blessing they have been in my life. I hope any and all with Fairview ties will more fully appreciate this place and will be reminded of their own blessings and experiences. I hope all of my readers, with or without Fairview ties, will be both entertained and inspired by my writing efforts. I hope everyone will laugh—or at least smile—and ponder, and come away grateful for the goodness of God and the blessings of the freedom and heritage we so abundantly share.

I will try to be as honest as I can, but I am taking some inspiration from Philosopher Pete, notary and postmaster from Ephraim, Utah, who reportedly said, "I haf read vat Brodder Yenson has written oond I can swear that it is the truth, de whole truth, oond yoost a little bit more dan de truth."[1] If you find anything I have written herein as "yoost a little bit more dan de truth," it is not a deliberate attempt to deceive. It is either a slight malfunction of my long-term memory (which at present is pretty good) or an attempt to tease you just a little and make you smile—I think you will know when.

To prompt my memory in researching for and preparing to write this memoir, I have walked every grave marker in the Fairview cemetery and driven every street in the community, with notebook in hand. I have conversed and reminisced with several people. I have also reviewed my school yearbooks, personal history, and other writings. These activities have brought me sweet remembrance of the many experiences I have had with the great folks of Sanpete County.

In referencing people, I generally use real names, but may take some liberties to protect both the innocent and the guilty. If I offend anyone, I am sorry.

In language, I try to generally tell it as I remember it. I was blessed to not often hear crude profanity in my youth, which I much appreciate. But, there seemed to be abundant *damns* and *hells,* and I will sometimes include them to be authentic to my experiences. These words, in my opinion, were perhaps a kind of a Mormon-culture substitute for more profane and graphic language—perhaps akin to Postum in lieu of coffee.

Welcome to a trek through my boyhood world of Fairview, Utah. I hope you will enjoy this journey and that may you be better for having taken it.

Reg Christensen
Waunakee, Wisconsin
2014

Chapter One:

Don't Cry Over Spilled Milk

One of my earliest memories of my maternal grandmother, Mary Malinda Peterson Tucker, was when I was perhaps five or six years old. My mother sent me walking the six blocks to her home before school to deliver a glass bottle of milk from our family cow. In my fumbling to open her door, I dropped the bottle, spewing glass and milk in all directions. I cried from my hurt pride and from disappointment that I had not accomplished my mission—one of the first solos of significant distance that my mother had entrusted to me. Grandma, with her perpetual smile, embraced me with her loving hugs and said, "Oh now, dearie, don't cry over spilled milk!" (Someone must have heard, because everyone was soon quoting her).

Grandma was born July 8, 1882, in Fairview and spent her entire life there. She and Grandpa lived in an old two-story frame house on the northwest corner, just east of the North ward stone church.

Grandma's hard scrabble life is incredible to me. She gave birth to eleven children, nine of whom lived to adulthood. She cooked on a coal stove, separated milk, churned butter, did laundry in a metal tub on a washboard, made laundry soap over an open fire in the yard, and pumped water from a well. Later, when they had a water line installed into the house, Grandpa joked with the plumber that he need not even attach a faucet, as she would "surely just use a steady stream." In the summer, they moved their large family into a tent in the mountains to be near Grandpa's work on the road and to graze their cows. Along with the unimaginable task of extended camping with her large brood, she set up her sewing shop and, with her old treadle sewing machine, made all of their school clothes.

On one occasion Grandpa came home with a new cabinet radio that he had purchased from Ed Garn, his district supervisor on the state road and the father of former US senator Jake Garn. Ed had somehow received possession of and was selling several of these radios, and Grandpa likely felt some pressure to purchase one. My mother used to tell of her memory of Grandma Tucker wiping the sweat from her brow as she scrubbed the laundry on the old worn washboard and saying, "I sure wish the hell Ed Garn sold washing machines."

Grandma had an eagle eye and a keen awareness of her surroundings. Occasionally in our home, she would point out that a particular picture or wall hanging was "just a tad off center." On another occasion, we were having a family spring cleaning of their home and property and Grandpa offered the old, disused outhouse to Kirby Bench, who wanted to install it on his out-of-town farm property. The men loaded it on Kirby's truck and hoped that he would get safely out of sight without Grandma seeing it. But no. In my mind, I can still see her running after the truck, hollering, "No, no—you can't have that!" (Kirby did not stop—most likely because he had no brakes on the truck. But the horn worked, so he was usually OK. At least that's what Dad taught me—you only need one or the other).

My fondest memories of Grandma came from the five years I served as her paper boy. I had conveniently organized my route around the town so Grandma's house was my halfway point. I would park my bike or hitch my horse to her fence and enter her warm and welcome home for a treat of hot chocolate and sugar cookies accompanied by abounding love and praise. Grandma was typical of so many striving Saints of the era who wanted to do right but struggled with abstinence from coffee. She would mix my chocolate and then fix herself a cup of hot water, as she called it, which had been brewed with just a tiny bit of coffee. My dad would tease her, "Grandma, you make your coffee so weak that you would have to drink four cups to even break the Word of Wisdom." With a playful twinkle in her eye, she would reply, "Oh, Boots, it's just hot water."

I loved the non-school days because I could linger at Grandma's long enough to get a double portion of love and cookies and make my remaining customers nervous about when they would receive their morning paper. One morning, I removed my boots and pressed my feet up against the warm outer shell of the old coal-fired Heatrola in the living room. When I did finally leave, the bottoms of my new insulated, rubberized socks stayed on the stove where they had melted completely off. The prints remained for years, always giving us a good laugh and a good memory of days gone by.

I had just turned thirteen when Grandma died on September 22, 1964, and I did not know quite how to deal with this first loss of a close loved one. I remember missing a whole week of school and spending time with my dad doing farm work in the fall. On the way home, we would stop to check in on Grandpa or to greet family. The emptiness in the big house was sadly oppressive, somewhat like the emptiness in my heart—mysterious and melancholy.

Uncle Jack later reported that Grandma's final words at her death in Utah Valley Hospital in Provo were in response to the noise of someone entering the hospital room. She stirred a bit and then said, "Oh, there is Reg with the paper!" And then she was gone—probably off to fix my hot chocolate and cookies and her hot water.

Chapter Two:

The Road Man

My maternal grandfather, Frances Marion Tucker, was also a birth-to-death resident of Fairview and expected that everyone would treat him accordingly. The story goes that he was once in a small fender-bender and when challenged for not using his turn signal, replied, "I have been turning on that corner for fifty years—everyone knows that!"

Grandpa was born on March 15, 1883. His father, Amasa—I have imagined him as perhaps a member of Nauvoo's Whistling and Whittling Brigade because he lived there at the appropriate age—was Fairview's first bishop, as so stated on the historical marker near the Peterson Dance Hall on Main Street.

Grandpa taught me a great lesson on being punctual and being prepared. When he went to court his gal, she was not ready, so he took out her sister instead—who subsequently became my grandmother. Grandpa was the road foreman for the Fairview Canyon road and ran a small family dairy. He hunted deer and elk to help feed his large family (I recall once when he was in his eighties and my brothers had shot one too many deer for their tags. They convinced Grandpa to go, bought him tags, put a rifle in his hands, and retrieved the deer. He seemed happily reminiscent of days gone by). His sons used to tease him because when he would point north at a deer, his finger was actually pointing mostly east. "Just where are you pointing, Dad?" they would jest. I believe that this was the result of an axe accident years earlier—probably one of those "just stop the bleeding and it should be fine" sort of things. He played baseball for the Fairview team. When I did the same years later, an old-timer commented to me that I played like my grandfather. Since I never saw him play, I have no idea whether or not this was meant as a compliment.

In his retirement years, he often managed the Skyline Motel for Uncle Keith and Aunt Ruby in their absence. He is renowned, with a healthy dose of humor, for when he diligently watered the artificial plants each day and also when he retrieved a small portable electric heater to warm a guest's room during a power outage.

After Grandma died, I became Grandpa's traveling companion on his journeys to Utah and Salt Lake Counties—mostly for medical visits. My job was to keep him safe. I recall being successful on at least one occasion when he passed a car on the winding roads through Birdseye. He mostly did fine but had an apparent memory lapse and, after passing, forgot to move back over into his own lane. I struggled with what to do and was finally prompted to action by an oncoming car, at which time I reached over and gently turned the steering wheel to move the car back into our lane. Several people—especially me—were relieved when I got my driver's license and he got his keys confiscated by his children. I became his chauffer.

On our journeys, I got better acquainted with him and even came to read his thoughts to some extent. For example, when he sent me to the store to buy him some Upjohn, he did not have to specify which of the hundreds of products he wanted—I knew it was laxative. When he talked about putting some new Kotex on the ceiling, I knew that he was referring to Celotex ceiling tile. He loved listening to basketball on his prized console radio and enjoyed the few times I took him to live games. I think he was disappointed that I was tall but not a basketball player. He was a musician—he sang in the church choirs and was one of the oft-featured musicians of the annual minstrel show productions. I still have a recording of him strumming his guitar and singing his old minstrel music to me and my wife when he was in his nineties. When I got married, I insisted that he come to the Manti Temple for the ceremony. He protested at how difficult it would be for him, but he still did.

Grandpa was adamant about not wanting to go to a nursing home. His children tried their best to care for him in his old age. We had him in our home for a while, but he just wanted to be home. The children took turns staying with him in his home until he died on August 24, 1978. I miss him and look forward to reuniting once again. I hope he got his crooked finger straightened out so he can point me in the right direction in the next world.

Chapter Three:
A Fish for Mother

I did not know either of my paternal grandparents in mortal life. I know very little of their personalities. Were they happy? Did they laugh often? The only photos I have seen are apparently from the time before smiling was invented, so they offer no clue. My grandmother, Johannah **Elenora**, was born in 1872 and died in 1926. My grandfather, Niels Peter, was born in 1867 and, as previously mentioned, died in 1951 just hours before I was born. I would like to think that perhaps we high-fived each other in the tunnel in passing, but I do not know. I do know that they had to be incredibly strong people to endure the trials they endured. What I know of these trials I learned from my father.

I write the remainder of this chapter about my grandparents in first person as though I were my father.

Although rural life seemed difficult for most in the early decades of the 1900s, my memories are of a charmed and exciting childhood. My father was employed as the construction foreman of the old Mammoth Reservoir, a water storage facility in the mountains a dozen or so miles east of our home in Fairview, Utah. This employment rewarded him well. In fact, one of my first recollections of my father was of him driving to our home with a new team of horses hitched to a new and brightly painted freight wagon loaded with wheat. This purchase, along with the rumor that he once had a thousand dollars, was the likely cause of some in the community giving him the nickname of "Rich Pete." His employ also allowed him to build my mother's beautiful new brick dream home—not too impressive by the standards of today, but certainly spacious and comfortable in that time and place.[2]

As I was born, the doctor could "find no life in me," but my Aunt Mary, still haunted by the early death of my older brother, defied death to also have me. She soon had me breathing and placed me on a pillow on the door of the warm oven to incubate me to life. I developed into a healthy and robust child who looked for adventure everywhere I could find it. As we lived for the summer months at the Mammoth construction site, my older siblings and I mined clay for the production of our toys and doll furniture and hiked the hills looking for beautiful flowers. We were frightened by a stray Holstein bull which free-roamed the mountain range. I was fascinated by the construction equipment and process and awed by the huge dam growing slowly out of the Gooseberry Narrows.

Our life back in town was comfortable in our nice home. My parents would sometimes roll back the rugs and, with their invited guests, enjoy a magical evening of dinner and dancing to the music of our new Victrola. Our home was near the railroad and the grain mill so I seemed to always have something new and exciting to see and do. I was to be the youngest of our large family and, as to be expected, was somewhat spoiled by my older brothers and sisters. Life was good.

And then, in an instant, everything changed. In June 1917, the terrifying, tragic news came to our community that the Mammoth Dam had collapsed. My father was in town at the time of the news, and as the newspaper later recalled, he "almost ruined a fast horse" in his attempt to get to the construction site. The ensuing flood killed one woman and washed out the railroads, thus interrupting the shipping operation of fourteen coal mines. This terrible event was followed by much speculation of what had gone wrong. As the event occurred during World War I, some of the engineers even purported sabotage by detonating a bomb in the water tower.

Over my lifetime, I have many times returned to the site of the tragedy. It has, for me, become somewhat of a sacred shrine because of the heritage it speaks of my father, and also because of the great moral lesson of life I see in the haunting ruins still looming above the stream bed. I have formed my own theory of the washout—that the foundation of the dam was not made sure upon the bedrock.

With the washout of the dam came also the washout of my father. Life became very difficult for him and Mother. Not only did he lose the secure job he had held for the previous decade, but he lost much of his self-esteem and confidence. My older brother later explained to me that the decision to pack up and move to Idaho was an attempt to keep my father from going insane. As life would be, the emigration to Idaho was merely a continuation of the spiral of hardship and trial.

Now that I am older, it makes me cry to imagine my mother storing the furniture and renting out their new home to leave for an unknown land. Oh, how she must have longed for her spacious, well-equipped kitchen as they pulled the old Model T out into the sagebrush to build a fire and cook their meals. What a dismal sight the old wooden granary must have been to her as they set up housekeeping there to await better lodgings someday. What heartache must have come as they realized the poor quality of the land they were attempting to homestead and make productive. How dark the world must have looked as our family was infected by the great flu pandemic in 1918. And yet there were those bright and shining stars of hope and charity, such as when a neighbor came and cared for us through our recovery and prevented us from needing to go, by order of the county, to one of the makeshift hospitals, where it seemed that "corpses were being carried out nearly as fast as patients were carried in."

The subsequent years brought further trial and disappointment. After abandoning the homestead land and now renting a farm, the sugar beet planting was thrice blown from the field before the plants could take firm root. Finally, the beets were abandoned in favor of a wheat crop that matured to a promising harvest. At the very hour the harvest was begun, the worst hailstorm of the decade ruined the entire crop.

Yet through it all was the indomitable will and faith of my mother. She made certain that we were loved and reassured. One day, after baking some pies for a neighbor, she and I mounted my pony to deliver them. I guess I sat too far back and got my feet in the pony's flanks. We were both bucked off as the pies smashed into the sand. She made sure that we both had a good laugh at our folly. That was Mother for you!

After a long struggle, Dad abandoned his efforts to tame the rugged soil. He and Mother packed up and returned to Utah where he found employment with the Utah Construction Company. Mother was delighted to be back in her new home. The years had passed and I was now thirteen. Life seemed good for my parents once again—but on the horizon was gathering the darkest cloud of my childhood. In the springtime, Mother was diagnosed with stomach cancer. She was soon taken to Salt Lake City for better medical care and I was sent to live with my sister and her family on their ranch about ten miles north of my home. I worried and prayed for my mother, but I did not know really of the seriousness of her illness. I had learned from her to make the best of all hard things and therefore had hope for her recovery.

My nephew and I would often fish the small river on the ranch. At one particular hole, a large clump of willows grew out over the bank. One day as I crawled out on the willows, I noticed a large fish basking lazily in the deep, clear pool. We tried for several days to entice this fish to our bait, but to no avail. Deep in my heart, I held a secret motive for wanting to catch the fish. My prayer was that I would be successful.

One day, I tried my usual methods of slowly pulling my bait near the fish, but he just ignored it. I then had the thought to hold the line in my fingers and twirl it, causing the bait to spin. This I did, as I moved it near his nose. This time, seemingly annoyed by the disturbance, the fish struck the bait and I had him hooked. I was so excited! I ran to the house where my sister helped me clean and prepare the fish. The next day, someone was going to Salt Lake and we sent along my trophy to my mother. Some days later, the news came back that my mother had not eaten any solid food in several days, but she had eaten and thoroughly enjoyed feasting on my catch. I was so happy that I was able to bring this joy into her life of suffering.

Some weeks later, Mother came home. I was over at the train depot when I saw her arrive and ran over, full of joy, to greet her. I was confident that she had come home to recover. I was not told that she had indeed come home to die in peace—the doctors could do nothing more for her. I was sent back to the ranch to stay with my sister. On one particular morning, I just felt that I needed to go home. I walked over to the railroad tracks and started to walk toward town. The railroad section crew soon came along on their motor car. In the past, they had often seen me playing near the tracks and had waved but never stopped to talk. This time they stopped. I told them that I needed to go home and the foreman sat me on the seat beside him and soon delivered me near my home. I ran in to see Mother. She had just lost consciousness. Dad wrote a note for me to take to my sister who lived in town. By the time we returned, Mother had passed away. This was the most terrible day of my life—my dear mother who had nurtured and taught me for so long was now gone. How could life go on without her?

Of course life does go on. I am grateful for wonderful brothers and sisters who provided homes for me and helped me learn of work and life and love. I am grateful for my father, who just kept plugging forward through life's trials. I enjoyed the brief times I had with him. I remember one time in particular when he and I and a few of my brothers returned to the Mammoth Dam site to demolish the buildings and salvage the lumber to be used in a construction project my brother was involved in. I could not help but wonder how my dad must have felt as he worked at dismantling what was once his kingdom. Life seems to be so full of mystery and uncertainty.

I suppose there are many things I am unsure of. I do not know for certain that Heavenly Father helped me catch the big fish for my mother—I would like to think that he did. I do not know if Mother really liked the fish as much as they told me she did, or if she just liked it because it was from her baby boy. I do not absolutely know that the Mammoth Dam failed because it was not built upon bedrock—it appears to me to be so. Were the railroad workers inspired to stop and pick me up the day my mother died? I believe they were. Did my mother hang on to life just long enough for me to see her and say my goodbyes? I hope so. Why did my mother have to die at this particular time of my life when we had already seemed to have had our quota of hardship? I do not know.

There are, however, a couple of things I do know with absolute certainty. I know that if we build and center our lives on the bedrock of Jesus Christ and His gospel, nothing will be wrong forever—our faith and eventual reconciliation need never wash away from us.[3] The Atonement will ultimately put everything right that could possibly go wrong in this world.

I also know that my mother and father loved me, and that I loved them.

Chapter Four:
The In-Between

My mother, Elna Fan Tucker Christensen, was fond of explaining to people that she was the "in-between" as she was number six of eleven children. She was born in Fairview on August 26, 1917, and except for a few short terms in a trailer house to be near her first husband's construction work, she lived in Fairview until she was eighty-four years old. She then came to Wisconsin so my family could care for her in her battle with Alzheimer's disease. During her first few months in the green, rolling hills of Wisconsin, she commented to everyone she met, "It is so beautiful here in the tops of the mountains!" After several attempts to explain to her that there are no mountains in southern Wisconsin, it occurred to me that it was my own reasoning that was bogus. If you live for eighty-four years in Fairview and look up at majestic mountains—and then you live where there are none—you must be "in the tops of the mountains." From then on, it made perfect sense.

When I was very young, Mom taught me the song of the meadowlark—"Fairview is a Pretty Little Town!" As I grew older and got out and about a bit, I learned that many other towns had apparently developed a sub-species of the Fairview meadowlark. I am amazed at the far migrations of these sweet-sounding birds—even to my current hometown, where they sing "Waunakee is a Pretty Little Town!"

Mom was a child of the Great Depression and a long-time member of the Daughters of the Utah Pioneers. She certainly carried on their legacy in deed as well as name. In the tradition of her own mother, she cooked our lye laundry soap over an open fire (I helped), churned our butter (or, rather, supervised me in churning our butter), quilted our quilts, and grew our vegetables. She wove our rugs on the Fairview South Ward rug loom (I collected and played with the empty spools), taught many others how to weave, conserved our resources, made do with what she had, washed our clothes in her old Dexter Twin-Tub, canned and stored what seemed like every edible thing she could get her hands on—she even pickled zucchini—and never wasted food, clothing, or anything else that I can recall. She often told of her joy and excitement as a child in receiving her very own orange in her Christmas stocking.

I do not ever remember hearing my mother offer a public prayer in church or give a talk or conduct any kind of a meeting. If she ever did, it was a certainly a very rare moment and likely terrified her to no end. But when someone was in need, she was—in the great Tucker tradition—often the first to arrive and the last to leave. She not only visited the distressed, the sick, and the dying, but she washed their dishes, laundered their clothes, scrubbed their floors, cooked their meals, tended their babies, ran their errands, and searched for ways to offer whatever help she could. Through it all, she shied away from any praise or accolade. She was naturally shy. In later years, when the folks of my Lehi ward would camp on our Fairview property, my dad would socialize with one and all. Often people would ask, "Is your mother still living?" I would assure them that she was and that she was likely at home working. In fact, they often enjoyed her sourdough pancakes but never met her. That is just who she was.

Mom seemed to accept people as they were and was willing to help them grow and progress. She often told of when she and her sister were employed as young girls to assist a local beekeeper. He instructed them to "go gather some chips," which she interpreted to be wood chips. When she returned with her chips, he laughed and instructed her that he meant cow chips for the smoker.[4] He then told her, "We all learn from the mistakes we make, girly, so go right ahead and make them." It seems that was her attitude with me when I once rushed to tell her that the toilet was overflowing, but dared not interrupt her back-fence conversation with our neighbor for quite some time. When I did speak, she flew into the house in a flash and put things right, with me as her helper. She was correct—I did learn from my mistake.

She seemed to have a great sense of timing in offering comfort. Once in the early springtime, I was rather distraught after receiving a scolding (well deserved, I am sure) from my neighbor for something I had done wrong. Mom had just found some of my Christmas gifts—stamp-collecting paraphernalia—that she had hidden and forgotten about months before. This belated Christmas gave me joy and comfort and helped ease the pain of my repentance.

On one occasion when I was older and had my young son with us, I went grocery shopping with Mom in Fairview. There we met Edda Graham and I delighted in introducing my first-grader to her and telling him that she had been my first-grade teacher. Mom informed us that Edda had also been her first-grade teacher. It is always so fun and awe-inspiring to weave the connections in our life tapestries.

After high school, Mom secured employment as a clerk in the Fairview post office. I am certain that she did her work, as in all things, with order and efficiency. She gained knowledge that remained with her for a lifetime. A few years before her death, I was driving her a few hours from Norma's home in Chicago to our home in Waunakee. To pass the time, I began randomly saying the names of cities throughout the United States to see if she could name the state where they were located. Even though her short-term memory seemed fried like a damaged circuit board, her long-term memory was as sharp as ever. She correctly identified the states of forty-eight of fifty-one cities I named. I asked her how she got to be so smart and she casually replied, "Oh, probably from my work in the post office."

She also got acquainted with a post office customer who was a heavy equipment operator and was in the area working on a road project. She and Charlie Bailey courted, fell in love, married, and had a son named Charlie. On little Charlie's second birthday, September 4, 1939, his dad was working on a construction project at Hill Air Force Base and Mom was in Fairview helping Uncle Jim and Aunt Geneva Larsen.[5] As Mom has told me the story, two men came to the door with an unwelcome task. One of the men, struggling for his words, said, "Mrs. Bailey, there has been an accident and Charlie has been hurt." The other man, apparently a charm school dropout, chimed in, "Hurt? Hell, he's dead!" So Mom now faced a new life trial of suddenly becoming a very young widow with a child to rear and an uncertain prospect of how to provide support. She was very grateful for her parents who were still alive and well and had true and loving hearts and willing hands.

Within a few years, Mom married my father. He was also a single parent struggling to rear a young son, Lowell. In fact, Charlie and Lowell were the same age. One of my boyhood delights was to tell people that I had "twin brothers, born four days apart" and then observe their reaction. I received a few condolences for Mom, as in, "Oh, your poor mother!" Mom and Dad then had three more children—Ron, Norma, and then me. So our yours-mine-and-ours family struggled along through smooth and rough times, but somehow survived—and all this in a day when bookstore shelves were not so replete with self-help guides for every circumstance.

Mom found her delight in simple matters. A few years before her death, I took her with me to visit a seminary class within my stewardship.

After driving for a few hours, I escorted her to the bathroom in the church. I knew it was vacant because it was dark when I opened the door and reached in to turn on the light for her. When she came out laughing, I asked what was so funny and she said, "There is a lady in there who is wearing the exact same dress that I am." Having learned by now not to try and reason with her, I just said, "Oh really? Well, what did you say to her?" Her reply: "We really didn't speak—we just looked at each other and laughed." When my mother looked in the mirror, she saw a sweet and genuine soul—even though she did not always recognize herself in her later life. But I knew who she was.

About lunchtime on February 28, 2008, I left my institute office to run a few errands and then drove to see Mom at the hospice center in Fitchburg, Wisconsin. When I was about two minutes away, Norma, who was with her, called to tell me she had just taken her last breath. I asked Norma to let me in the back door near her room and we just sat and reminisced for a while. The mortuary people then arrived and we walked with them alongside the gurney through the long halls to the front door while all the staff stood in silent respect with bowed heads. One young man caught our eye and offered a reverent smile—he had worked as a nurse for Mom in her care center for several months before she came to hospice and knew there was much about her life that warranted joy.

One of Mom's concerns during her final years was that she wanted to be buried in Fairview. Ron had exacerbated her concern over the years by kidding her, "You won't have a thing to say about it!" The matter of her burial became particularly important to her as she was uprooted from her lifelong home and transported to Wisconsin (She got a fortune cookie shortly after her arrival that said "You will spend your golden years in a strange land." In all fairness, I do not recall if it really said that or if that is just how I read it to her. I suspect the latter). We honored her wish and transported her body back to Fairview where she was buried in the Tucker family plot beside her beloved Charlie.

Chapter Five:

The Prankster

When Curly Swenson and his wife went out of town for a week or so, he asked my dad to care for his old mongrel dog. One day when Dad went to their house, it snapped at him. This started the wheels turning in Dad's mind—although I am not sure they were ever idle when it came to stuff like this. He took great care to cut a tombstone shape from an old wood scrap. He then hauled dirt to Swensons' front lawn and formed a small grave mound. On the day of the Swensons' return, he locked the dog way back in the furthest shed behind the house. When they arrived, they were bewildered at no greeting from their dog and then at the tombstone with the epitaph, "Here lies Big Red—Yesterday he bit me and today he is dead!" That was Dad—a perpetual prankster of the highest order.

My dad, Rob Buford Christensen, was born in Fairview on May 25, 1913. My sister, Norma, had it in her mind for most of her early life that his first name was Robert—she even listed it such on her wedding announcements. I broke the news to her by saying, "Hey, if your name were Robert, would you go by Buford?" Dad laughed about it all. I am uncertain as to how he got the nickname "Boots," but I would logically surmise that it came from someone who observed that he often wore his irrigation boots—sometimes knee length and sometimes hip length—all around the town.

From the time of his mother's early death when Dad was thirteen, he was cared for by various relatives. One result of the failed attempt by his parents at homesteading land in Rupert, Idaho, was that my Uncle Ed, Dad's older brother, settled there permanently and Dad lived with his family for a time—playing football for and then graduating from Rupert High School. Dad often recounted with fondness and longing the days after high school when he worked for the Laidlaw Sheep Ranch in Idaho.

Idaho was good to Dad. I recall reading John Steinbeck's *The Grapes of Wrath* and being sickened by the heartless cruelty, inhospitality, deceit, and abuse heaped upon the Dust Bowl refugees migrating to the West Coast. One morning I had a great conversation with Dad about this same era in his life and how he and a few other young men from Fairview went to Idaho seeking work. He spoke with gratitude of a farmer who let them camp in his orchard and help themselves to some fruit and vegetables while they got established.

Although we as a family have maintained permanent ties to Rupert—my brother Lowell permanently settled there—Dad returned to his Fairview roots. He worked hard at various things and developed his talents. For a time, he ran a service station on the southeast corner of State and Center Streets. Later, when I was young, he operated the old Phillips 66 station at the north end of town for a short while.[6] When people asked me what my father did during the war, I was not sure but later learned that he was on an agricultural deferment for his grain cleaning business, which he ran for several years. He worked as a carpenter and a concrete man—I still see his imprint on some of the concrete weirs of the old Fairview irrigation system. Through it all, he operated our small farm in the foothills just north of the Fairview Canyon road.

Dad got an opportunity to work in the insurance business and did so successfully for a few decades. He regularly purchased a new car and then wore it down traversing the highways and small towns of southern Utah, often stopping at a sheep camp or a remote home at the end of a lane to get acquainted with new friends and sell them life insurance. His personable, outgoing nature made him a natural for this work.

Dad fell in love with and married a Fairview gal—Anna Laura Turpin. Their names are still carved in a memorial heart in the sandstone cliffs just over the San Pitch River from the Turpin farm south of Fairview. I grew up referring to Anna Laura's mother, Caroline, as my grandmother—even though she wasn't really. She lived just around the corner from us and she occasionally tended me.[7] I loved to visit her home and see the many beautiful quilts she made. I also called Anna Laura's brother and his wife, Clarence and Fern, my uncle and aunt, and their children—Robin, Kevin, Wayne, Howard, and Stanley—my cousins. I spent much of my youth working with them on their dairy.

Dad and Anna Laura had a baby boy, Lowell, who barely lived but, as with my father, those attending him would not give up on his life. Just like Dad, they incubated Lowell on the oven door and restored him to life. They were not so fortunate with Anna Laura, who died on September 15, 1939, just one week after giving birth to Lowell. Life was dark and difficult once again for Dad. Many helpful friends and relatives pitched in and cared for baby Lowell while Dad worked to provide for his son and figure out his future. In a few years, he married my mother and they went forward together in the rearing of their "twin" boys.

By the time I was old enough to be out and about with Dad, the older boys were moving on, so I became his little pal. He would occasionally buy me a Best Pal candy bar. More than the candy, I loved how he gave it to me—"This is for my best pal!" I spent much of my youth riding straddle as a sort of hood ornament on our old 8N Ford tractor as we farmed and rode around the town plowing snow for people in winter. I recall one summer when we had worked our fourteen-acre farm by the San Pitch River northwest of town until it was too dark to see. As we drove home down the back streets, I was at my usual perch on the tractor hood when, just as we passed Val Tucker's home, the sky lit up like daytime. We watched for some moments as a huge comet traversed the sky in incredible splendor. When the event was recounted in the news, I felt privileged to have been there as an eyewitness and marveled as to why they did not interview me since I was certain that it landed in our fields we had just left—although I could never find it.

Dad almost always wore old bib overalls and a straw hat—or on special occasions, new bib overalls and a new straw hat. When Mom, Dad, Norma, and I were once traveling through southern Utah, we visited the Glen Canyon Dam. Dad did not have the proper change for the tour down inside to view the generators, so he paid with a twenty and the agent said she would catch him coming back to give him his change. As we were approaching the booth on our way out, the agent called out, "Mr. Christensen, I have your change." Dad asked, "Now, how do you think she could recognize me so quickly in this crowd of people?" I replied, "Dad, look around. How many other men do you see wearing bib overalls and a straw hat?"

Dad spoke his mind, often with humor, which I think was generally well received and sometimes gave him a payoff. On one very early morning (about 4:00 a.m). and very rare occasion, the highway patrol had set up a roadblock/checkpoint on Main Street just as Dad was returning from changing the irrigation water at the farm in Lowell's old Model A Ford. He pulled up to the attending officer, Bert Weldon, and stuck his arms out the window with both wrists together. Burt said, "What are you up to, Boots?" Dad replied, "Well, sir, I am driving an unlicensed vehicle with no working lights, no horn, and no brakes; do not have my driver's license: and do not have my glasses. So you just as well go ahead and put the handcuffs on me." Burt replied, "Boots, get this jalopy home before a cop catches you!"

Years later, Dad and Mom were returning home after visiting my family in Lehi. They had Grandma Cox from Ephraim with them. They had just entered the freeway when a policeman pulled Dad over for driving too slow. After examining his license and registration, the officer came to the window and said, "Mr. Christensen, you were driving too slow and your car license has expired by three months." Dad said, "Aw hell, we don't worry about that kind of stuff down where I live," and continued in similar banter with the officer. The officer good-naturedly assured him that they did worry about it there and gave him a citation—but, in the end, all were in good humor. When we saw Grandma Cox again, she laughed so hard she could barely tell us the story.

On one occasion, Dad—prompted by the inaccuracy of the TV weather reports—carved a wooden "weather mule," complete with a rope tail. He then mailed it to Dick Nourse, the popular Channel 5 TV news anchor and asked him to present it on air to Bob Welti, the weatherman. Dick did so. I recall Dad's joy and excitement when Dick Nourse introduced the weather portion of the broadcast by saying something like "We have a special presentation for Bob from Boots Christensen down in Fairview, who hopes this weather mule will help him be more accurate with his reporting. Boots writes, 'If tail is horizontal—wind. If tail is dripping water—rain. If mule is white—snow.'" Dad's hours constructing the weather mule paid him big returns as his friends in the community laughed and praised him for his innovation.

Dad never lost his love for old things and times past. Throughout his life, he maintained his hobby of restoring and driving old horse-drawn wagons and buggies. He would explore an old shed or barnyard, find the metal frame of a deteriorated buggy, negotiate with the owner for its possession, and then begin the process of restoration. Until his older years, he always maintained a team of horses to pull his wagons in the summer and bobsled in the winter. In my young married years, I became his helper to transport buggy and horses to the local parades and events. He delighted in escorting Santa Claus or a grand marshal in one of his buggies or giving rides to his many visitors on such occasions.

Dad often offered his non-politically correct assessment of community and world happenings. When Fairview City assessed a special tax to build a museum to house a replica of the wooly mammoth found in the excavation of Huntington Reservoir Dam, Dad told one and all, "I wish they had never found that damned elephant!" Shortly after the Arab oil embargo of the mid-seventies when I brought my Lehi ward to our Fairview property to camp, Dad was the self-appointed welcoming committee. As folks would arrive in their fancy trailer homes and campers, he would drive his horses and buckboard around greeting each guest with, "Tell the Arabs to go to hell!" (My Lehi friends still talk about it). On more than one occasion, I heard him tease his friends, Bernard and Laura Turpin, "How did a homely old couple like you get such a pretty daughter?" Whenever someone asked "Don't I know you from someplace?" he would delight in replying, "You sure do—don't you remember that we were cellmates at Alcatraz? Let's see, what were you in for?" (Years later, I picked up on this little prank—substituting "county jail" for the now-defunct Alcatraz. One evening while at dinner in Salt Lake with my children, a man approached our table and expressed that he thought he knew me. I gave him the old line, "Yes, from county jail," to which he replied, "Hmm, I do not remember arresting you." It turned out that he was one of my former seminary students—and now an undercover cop).

Dad seemed to have a gift for messing with people's minds. He once brought a brown cultured-marble figure of a gorilla home and gave it to my mother, telling her it was chocolate. She hid it deep in the fridge in order to resist the urge to eat it, as once she started, she know she would likely consume it all. When she finally did give in, she thought she would just taste it by cutting off an ear with the butcher knife. Finding out the truth when it could not be cut, she threatened to turn the knife on Dad.

I was with Dad once in the Fairview grocery store when we went through a particularly busy checkout line. When the clerk asked how she could help him, he handed her a twenty-dollar bill and asked if she could just change it for him. She assured him that she could and asked what he wanted. He replied, "Oh, two tens and two fives would be fine." She obliged. We then stood in the corner by the front exit door for a while until she realized what she had done—"Dang you, Boots!" I was amazed that they did not ban him from the store, as he would sometimes move a lady's purse to someone else's cart or slip a six-pack of beer or a carton of cigarettes into the cart of an unsuspecting bishop's wife or temple worker and then follow them through the checkout so he could hear them sputter at the discovery. But, they all knew Dad and all was taken in good fun.

In Dad's later years, he and Mom were called as temple workers. Just before their ride picked them up one morning, Dad's wallet had dropped into the toilet, so when their friends came to the door, Dad was ironing his money. He announced that he had to finish his "money laundering" before they could go. At the temple one afternoon, the president stopped at the easy chair Dad had found and asked, "Well, Brother Christensen, what service are you doing in the Lord's house today?" Dad answered, "Oh, I have been busy—I just need to rest for a while." The temple president said, "Well, thank you for your service. What have you been doing?" Dad replied, "Oh, I have been busy—they have had me cleaning and polishing all of the ashtrays throughout the entire temple!"

My friends who only knew one side of Dad were incredulous when I told them he struggled with depression—particularly in his later years. Perhaps the pranks and humor were somewhat of a mask for his deep sorrows and trials. Nevertheless, he endured and tried to keep plugging along. In his final months, Mom was determined to keep him at home as long as possible. When I first realized what a struggle this was for her, I became more involved in his care. I would travel to Fairview a few nights each week to give Mom a respite and then return to Lehi in the early mornings to teach seminary and fulfill my family and bishop responsibilities.

On one particularly difficult night, I just could not seem to do anything to get Dad to settle down. He seemed crazy. He scolded me with, "How can you do this to me? How can you make me work out here in this wet cement when I am not feeling well?" A few hours later, the scolding was aimed at Charlie, who was not even there: "Charlie, don't give those good oats to that worthless old horse!"

I finally got an idea. I said, "Dad, are you ready to die?" He calmed and seemed to ponder this question long and hard and then said, "Yes, I think so." I said, "Well, Norma is on her way from Chicago and will be here tomorrow night. Wait until she gets here to see you and then go ahead and die if you want to." He did. She arrived on Monday evening. On Tuesday, he slipped into unconsciousness and died on Friday, January 31, 1997, at age eighty-three. He was buried in the Fairview Cemetery beside his beloved Anna Laura. Wouldn't you know they spelled his name wrong on the tombstone—"Bufford" rather than "Buford." Sometimes I think about getting it corrected, but then I consider that Dad would not much care—and probably accepts it as some sort of prank or payback. Perhaps it was.

Chapter Six:
Fairview is a Pretty Little Town

Well, back to that meadowlark. Yes, Fairview is a "pretty little town" nestled in the western valleys of the majestic mountains of the Manti-La Sal National Forest. There were—and still are—many blessings from being off the proverbial beaten path. For example, the smog of the more northern cities of the Wasatch Front doesn't seem to find its way to Sanpete. The sunlight does seem to make it, although Dad loved to tell folks, "We are so far back in the hills that they have to pipe the sunshine to us." But, you must understand Dad. He loved Fairview, but he also loved poking all the fun he could at himself and his fellow citizens. I have often heard him tell folks his account of the settlement of Fairview, which went something like this: "When Brother Brigham was settling the Utah Territory, he sent scouts down through the valleys to look for settlement sites. In north Sanpete, they constructed signs stating 'Go East!' at the western mouth of each canyon. When the settlers came through North Bend (later named Fairview), those who could read went east, and the rest of us are still here." And alas, even Brother Brigham was not exempt from Dad's fun. As we stood on a street corner in Salt Lake once when I was small, Dad pointed out the statue of Brigham in the intersection, standing with his back to Temple Square and his out-stretched arm signifying, "This is the place!" Dad recited to me, "There he stands upon his perch, his hand toward the bank and his back toward the Church." Dad was not apostate—just a comic.

In former times, a tri-weekly passenger train served the Sanpete Valley. Dad's interpretation was that "It would try one week to return by the next." I loved his story—probably apocryphal—of a sleepy workman returning home from Salt Lake on a Friday evening via the tri-weekly and giving strict instructions to the porter to "make sure I get off this train in Fairview even if you have to throw me off!" It did not happen. When they pulled into Salina, the man woke up, and realizing how far he had overshot his destination, cursed and yelled at the porter as he exited the train. To the chagrined porter, a passenger commented, "Oh my, that was sure an angry man!" The porter replied, "Yes sir, he was—but if you think that was something, you should have seen the man I threw off in Fairview." I love the rich folklore of Sanpete.

Since I have been gone from Fairview for about forty-five years, a drive to Fairview (which I try to make several times a year) is, for me, a memorable journey through my former life. As I leave Spanish Fork and approach the mouth of the canyon on Highway 89, I have a vivid memory of the old Trojan explosives plant huddled against the east mountains. I recall a time when I was at our little league baseball practice in Fairview and word came through our grapevine that a man who lived just up the street had been killed in an explosion at the plant, rousing the vivid imaginations of our group of young boys.

Driving on through Thistle, I contemplate the eerie geology of this place. It appears as though entire mountains were picked up and jammed at strange angles back into the earth. I can't help but think of the land destruction at the time of the Crucifixion when "rocks were rent" and "the face of the whole earth" was broken up and thereafter found in "seams and cracks."[8] Testament to the instability of the area was offered by the Thistle landslide of 1983, when an entire mountainside slipped and dammed the Spanish Fork River, creating a destructive lake that pretty much destroyed whatever was left of Thistle—which wasn't much really, except to those few who still had homes there. I notice that the old red rock schoolhouse is mostly gone now. There wasn't much of it left even when I was a boy.

Beyond Thistle is Birdseye, with its little white church surrounded by red dirt and rocks. Once, just as we were driving by, Santa Claus descended from the rocks in his bright red suit, crossed the highway, and entered the white church. The red color of the dirt and rocks came from blood spilled in the great Indian Wars—at least, that was Dad's explanation to me. The massacre of the Given family certainly adds an eerie mystique to his theory. I occasionally stop to read the historical marker of this event on the east of the highway at the north end of the Indianola meadows. On May 26, 1865, John Given, his wife, Eliza, and their four children were brutally massacred by Indians. Two men working for the Givens escaped and ran for help, but returned too late to save them. The entire family is buried in Fairview. My sister, Norma, and I used to visit and place flowers at the grave each year on Memorial Day.

Much of Fairview is about as it was when I lived there. Dad's opening line in a letter to me while I was on my mission stated, "Well, there is not much new here—except that the manure piles are a little higher." The old rock house where Mom learned of the death of her first husband still stands. The old post office and the old library have been recently razed at the time of this writing.. The old Peterson dance hall still stands and has been beautifully restored. I was grateful for a recent tour of the place given by my friend Ed. A pre-remodeled portion of the South Ward church building is enough as it was when I attended there to spark many fond memories. The home we grew up in has changed colors but still stands and speaks sweet reminiscence. The buildings that housed Floyd's Drug Store, the Travel Inn Café, and Orson's Barber Shop still stand—but I do not know what they are at present. I vividly remember the day that the new Fred's Café opened at the north end of Main Street and how excited I was to ride my bike there to purchase what was perhaps the first malt made by Freddy in his new business. It is still a café. The drive-in next door—formerly Curly's—sparks fond memories from my own children of when their Grandpa Boots drove them through the drive-up window in his horse-drawn buggy to buy them ice cream. Across the street from Fred's was the Skyline Motel, operated by Uncle Keith and Aunt Ruby. The buildings for Mack's Garage and Wen's Service still stand but now serve different purposes.

From the valley, I can look up to our old farm and still see the monstrous deer stand built by my brother Ron. From his position in this mega-watchtower, the deer stood little chance of escape. The old feed mill in town still stands, as does the home built by my Christensen grandparents just to the west across the tracks and the road from the feed mill.

Although some structures are gone, they are still vivid in my memory. Just down the street from the home of my Christensen grandparents was the home of my Tucker grandparents. This old two-story frame home has been replaced by the home of my cousin Marion. Rod's Grocery, Peterson Hardware, and Carlson's Grocery used to operate on the block that is now CentraCom. At the other end of that block and on the west was Sanderson's Mercantile.

On the north side of the canyon road just before the entrance to our farm lane was the old two-story red brick county infirmary—the "Poor House," as my folks called it (I only remember it as a haunted house). I was fascinated by the many stories my folks told me of its residents, such as one old man who would stick to whatever task given him until someone made him stop (I would think they had to be a bit cautious about having him milk the cow). I recall telling Dad that I wish the man still lived so we could have him help us pick up rocks from our farm fields.

I notice that some of the buildings of Hansen Lumber and Sawmill are still there, but gone is the sawmill itself, where Uncle Keith tried to kill me by working me to death.

Entering town from the northwest, we cross the San Pitch River[9]—the source of so much boyhood fun and adventure. South of town is Spring Creek, where I tried so hard to catch fish but never with much success. A drive up Fairview Canyon brings a flood of memories of my own life and of the lives of my parents and grandparents, who had such rich experiences in these pristine and beautiful mountains.

As I drive around town and see the homes, some of which I easily recognize, I think of the people. I knew most of them from being their paperboy for several years. Now they are mostly laid to rest in the cemetery. As I meander through the cemetery, I have two vivid memories. One is of a photo contest I entered from a newspaper ad and was sure I would win, even though I do not think I had ever taken a photo before. I borrowed my mother's camera and rode my bike to the cemetery, where I took a single photo of the whole of Fairview lying peaceful and serene at the base of snow-covered mountains. I do not think the contest people ever responded to my entry, but I have never forgotten the incident and often see this impression of beautiful Fairview in my mind's eye.

My second memory is much more eternal and significant. It is of the many great souls of Fairview—some still living and some whose names are carved on the tombstones. Each has influenced and inspired my life, for which I am grateful. If I were to randomly name just a few of them as a representative sample of so many, I would list Wen, Ruby, Mack, Clarence, Floyd, Ida, A.J., Edda, Gary, Leon, Reed, Byron, Lillian, Keith, Winne, Jerry, VanNoy, Iven, Gloria, Albert, Stella, Don, Hazel, Larry, Frank, Woody, Edith, Gene, Reva, Blaine, Margaret, Clyde, Lucille, Kirby, Henry, Fern, Sherrill, Bill, Lucy, Otis, Alice, Darrell, Ethel, Glade, LeAnn, Shirley, Ross, Brent, Lloyd, Loa, and so many more!

And then if I were to name a random sampling of those closer to my own age representative of so many for whom I am grateful[10]— just a few of whom currently have names on grave markers—I would say Rian, Tim, Kip, Laurel, Lesa, Ruth, Mike, Dixie, Marelle, Curtis, Lona, John, Kim, Ed, Joann, Mark, David, Vangie, Eric, Jackie, Kurt, Sharene, Randy, Kevin, Branch, Wally, Sherrie, Ken, Roger, Jim, Corey, Bonnie, Ralph, Pam, Eddy, Hazel, Karl, Karen, and Leon.

To me, Fairview is a pretty little town, not as much for its physical setting and ambiance—as impressive as that is—but more so because of the beautiful people who have, at one time or another, chosen this heavenly place as their earthly home.

Chapter Seven:

A Mayberry Kinship

Some of my friends and family—particularly my children—have puzzled over the years as to my sense of kinship and fascination with *The Andy Griffith Show*. They have likely wondered why a relatively sane and mature adult man would be so drawn to such an overly simplistic TV program about a small town full of simple folks, including some very eccentric personalities. The answer is that I, in a figurative sense, grew up in Mayberry. In so stating, I am in no way insulting Fairview, and I try to not overemphasize the eccentricities—but I share many. Fairview, unlike Mayberry, was and is a very real place with very real challenges, heartaches, and joys. But like Mayberry, we tried to keep the world somewhat at bay. People cared for one another and helped safeguard the common good of the community. We felt safe in our town. We felt free to work hard, play hard, and laugh and cry at our circumstances.

The fact that our local sheriff carried no gun, plainly spoke reason and common sense to folks, and chased down speeding cars in his personal bright orange antiquated pickup truck, which he hurriedly outfitted with a flashing light on top as he began his chase, may have seemed strange to the many passers-through that he stopped in front of my home, but we natives took it all in stride. We were just glad that he was out there doing his job and making our community better. Plus, he benefitted the violators by causing them to slow down just a bit and take note of the good place they were in.

I wish I could go back and reminisce with one California family who drove through in the middle of the night and had their car broadsided at the intersection near our home by what was probably the only other moving vehicle in town at the moment. Although cars were totaled, gratefully no one was seriously injured. Dad was first at the scene and, along with other locals, gave the family a generous dose of small town hospitality, offering food, lodging, friendship and whatever else was needed over several days as they put life back together. I was surprised they didn't just stay in Fairview—perhaps they considered it.

We didn't depend much on social programs to right all of our wrongs and sometimes life just was not fair—but we survived. When VanNoy's service station got toilet papered one night, he served justice by having me clean it all up when I delivered his morning paper, serving proxy for the unknown real culprit. When I accidentally threw the morning paper through Moroni Vance's front window, I rationalized that maybe he was still asleep and wouldn't notice and went on my way. When I got home, Dad was already gathering up tools after receiving a phone call. He took me immediately back to the house where he and Moroni, with no scolding that I recall, taught me how to set and glaze a new window glass, funded from my earnings.

Officer Bill chased me down into my own driveway in his orange truck for driving my motorbike without a license. When he asked me if I had one, I sheepishly replied, "Yes . . . a fishing license." I was momentarily convinced that I was being honest. He didn't let me get away with it and gave me a good scolding that motivated me to change my wicked ways. There was no appeal provision that I recall in the court of Officer Bill. Sometimes the sense of fair play got distorted just a bit, like when old Willis was traveling with his wife and friends in southern Utah and their restaurant served up some spoiled beans. Willis said to the others, "Well, we have ordered them now so we will have to eat them."

My brother Ron knew the hometown culture well enough that when he was in the army in France, he inserted a line smack in the middle of a postcard home: "Oh, hello Uncle Jack. How are you doing?" Uncle Jack was the assistant postmaster and was genuinely interested in his nephew (Uncle Jack told us about reading the postcard with not a bit of embarrassment, only good humor). We had a party-line phone system with sometimes two to four people on the same line. We knew that if we quietly and carefully picked up the phone, we could listen in to the conversations of our neighbors, who sometimes spoke more cautiously and sometimes not, just accepting it as it was.

My young life seemed full of fascination and mystery. When I had a wart, Dad took me to visit Witch Mary so I could give her a penny and hear whatever it was she had to say to me. My wart soon disappeared. As I got my hair cut at Orson's Barbershop, I often tried to figure out a way to sneak into the back room to see if there was a body attached to the deer head and antlers hanging on the other side of the wall. Each month as I would collect for the newspaper from Pete, I wondered with wide-eyed curiosity about the pirate wars he may have fought in as he counted out the bills to me with his hooked arm. When the city workers cut down a huge cottonwood tree near our home, we delighted for days in playing among the hidden caverns and caves formed by the felled branches.

I marveled in visiting Lee's Meat Locker. We would retrieve packaged meat from our stash and enter the huge freezer with all of the eerie carcasses hanging on the racks. At Sanderson's Mercantile, Carlson's Grocery, Rod's Meat Market, and Peterson Hardware, I often drooled at the exotic fruits and foodstuffs and interesting gadgets and tools for sale. Virgil even gave me possession of a shiny new bicycle when I gave him half down and promised to go in each week thereafter to pay the balance from my newspapers and other earnings. I kept a meticulous record. When his clerk failed to record one payment, Virgil took my word for it and credited my account the next week when I presented my ledger. I liked being trusted. I could hardly believe my good fortune on the few rare occasions when my frantic bike rides actually brought me to the fish truck just as it was dumping its cargo of young fish into the San Pitch. More often than not, it headed up the canyon for the lakes and streams and I could not catch up, even with my new bike.

We worked. Aunt Ruby corralled me into the 4-H program where I learned to garden and taught leather tooling to a group of younger children. I was shadow to Dad and his many farm chores and projects, and I was his junior business partner in the construction and management of the Wagon Wheel Trailer Park and Laundry. I was so excited when Woody delivered our lumber with his big truck and my father and I built the building that would house our business (The building stands next to the Steven Bench dental office). Mom always found plenty of chores for me to do, like helping her make lye soap over a fire in the backyard, churning the butter, and scrubbing the wallpaper. For most of my youth, I managed a newspaper route, and for a few of the years, I delivered both the morning and the evening papers. I always delivered the Sunday paper through Oak Creek and Milburn. My sister, Norma, contends that I still have the first dollar I ever earned, to which I replied, "No, but I probably have a ledger account of how I spent it."

We played. We loved sledding on Ruel's lane, our farm lane, or the canyon road. Dad often said of me, "On the last day of school, he would stop at the barber and get his hair cut off, discard his shoes, and run wild until fall when we would catch him, put his shoes back on, and send him back to school." Except for the fact that I generally wore shoes, his statement rings mostly true. We often camped—usually in our backyards—and I would sometimes arise in the middle of the night and deliver my papers so we could hike to the San Pitch for fishing at first light. I spent countless hours patrolling the community on my horse, pretending to be the Lone Ranger battling the forces of evil for the cause of truth. What is now the large parking lot of the old South Ward church building was our sandlot football and baseball field. For a while, I became a pinball wizard at the Travel Inn Café until Don Ramey, the proprietor, saved my soul by suggesting that I not play quite so much. One night each week, the Peterson Dance Hall was opened for roller skating with Alt Jones keeping us in line and repairing the old clamp-on skates we rented and pushed to the limits with our wild skating games around the hall. We played little league baseball. We "played out"—a term I have suspected as rather original to Fairview (My own children later called it "night games"). We played "No Bears Are Out Tonight," "Run, Sheep Run," "Hide and Seek," and "Kick the Can." We played on the simple slides and swings at the city park and spent hours on the old tennis court. If you hit a ball over or through the tennis court's chicken wire enclosure, a treasure hunt ensued until it was found in the tall weeds surrounding it. I sometimes rode my bike six miles to Mt. Pleasant to the nearest swimming pool. I built my own high jump pit with wooden posts, a long piece of wood as the crossbar, and sawmill shavings from Uncle Keith as the cushioning for the landing pit. We dug underground houses where we squirrelled away our treats of apples and plums.

On one very memorable Saturday, our Cub Scout pack went to the Salt Lake International Airport to watch the planes taking off and landing. Then, to our extreme delight, we actually got to board an airplane and walk down the aisles and even sit for a moment and pretend that we were soaring off into the wild blue yonder.[11] After our airport visit, we, along with a couple of parents as chaperones, boarded a passenger train in Salt Lake and rode all the way to the Thistle junction where our parents met us for the drive home. This was a very exciting day!

Dad occasionally reminded me that it was sometimes possible to learn more out of school than in school. I loved when he checked me out of school because the combine was coming to harvest our wheat or when we cut Christmas trees or cedar posts for a church fundraiser or went to the coal mine to haul home our winter coal. These were wonderful days!

I felt I had entered a new world of intrigue and fascination when Dad and I would visit our old friend Lyndon Graham and watch his progress on his intricate carvings of everything from the Taj Mahal to a historic funeral coach. He also showed us his arrowheads and other Indian artifacts he had gathered from the local area and delighted us with his stories. His work is now on display at the Fairview Museum for all to enjoy.

We performed. Under direction of Eda Anderson, we traveled each year to the other north Sanpete communities with our road show. One year, I was a bruised and tattered Uncle Sam—rejuvenated by a patriotic rebirth, illustrated by the pulling of several strings that yanked off my black eye, my arm bandage and my head wrap as I stretched and stood up tall and proud. In a Primary production, I was once assigned the role of the big bad wolf in the epic *Three Little Pigs*. I wore a long fur coat and some type of papier-mâché head that got stuck in the cooking pot as I came down the chimney—thus adding a whole new dimension to the performance.

In Cub Scouts, we performed a skit dressed as a bunch of hillbillies sitting on the ground near a railroad track and passing back and forth the question of whether or not any trains were coming. We drew it out good and long with inquiry of trains from the east, west, north, and south before we finally served up our punch line: "Well then, I reckon we can cross the tracks." One summer, we assembled a dance team for June Conference in Salt Lake where, in full costume, we danced the Salty Dog Rag with what seemed like a million other dancers from around the state. In high school, I was a sword dancer in *Brigadoon*, and often wish I had pursued other roles in other plays—but life does move forward.

Does all of this help explain my affinity to Mayberry? What I like about Mayberry and about Fairview is the basic, old-fashioned goodness of the many people I knew and loved and the simple and pure activities of life that often seem so distant from our modern, noisy world.

Chapter Eight:
The Scream Heard Around the Town

I am honestly not sure how most of the Fairview folks felt about the changing world we lived in during my years growing up. I would suppose that some welcomed the future and were happy to hasten it. Others were likely content with the status quo, and I am sure others would have turned the clock back if they could have.

Dad was of the latter mindset. Some of his happiest moments were spent reminiscing about his employment as a young man for the Laidlaw sheep ranch in Idaho. He was calmed by his hobby of restoring old horse-drawn wagons and buggies. He and I shared many joyful hours of visiting the old folks of our community, both relatives and non-relatives, and hearing their memories of an earlier, simpler era. In hindsight, I acknowledge how much I have been influenced by this aspect of my youth—I seem very at home with old folks. This created a sort of strange ambivalence with my chosen profession of teaching youth. And yet the two worlds have often merged comfortably together as I used personal stories and examples from a time long ago and a place far away in my teaching. One day, Dad and his comical old Fairview friend dropped unexpectedly into the seminary class I was teaching, arrayed in their trademark bib overalls, and just sat down in the desks like they belonged there. I pulled them into the discussion and prompted them to share examples from when they were teens. The class of young freshmen loved it and talked about it for weeks to come.

Within a few days after my fifth birthday on September 1, 1956, we experienced the rare excitement of having the threshers come to our home and thresh our wheat. Modern combines were well in use by then, but this was Dad's world and his operation, and he wanted to grow and bind and thresh our own wheat. Earlier in the year, we had purchased an old grain binder in Idaho, transported it to our farm, and tuned it up to fair working condition.[12] I do not recall who owned and operated the threshing machine, but would guess that this was perhaps one of the last times it was used. We used our binder for only this one harvest.

Thereafter, it sat in the trees at the farm and served as one of my favorite toys. It may still be sitting there today. I remember sitting on the seat for hours, imagining it to be some sort of a fighter plane or pirate ship or perhaps even a grain binder, with me as its skilled pilot, captain, or operator.

My memory of my actual birthday is vivid. It was such a full day of wonder and excitement. There were, of course, candles to blow out and cake to eat, and also a visit to Doc Madsen for a mandatory physical so I could start school. But most exciting of all was the wheat harvest in progress. I just wanted to live every moment of it and be a part of each phase. I pestered my mother to get me home quickly from the doctor so I could return to my adventures.

As we pulled into our driveway, Dad and one of my brothers were backing a freshly loaded wagon of grain sheaves into our garage to protect the grain from a pending rainstorm. The wagon was a two-wheeled contrivance hitched to the tow bar of our little 8N Ford tractor. This bar could be raised or lowered by the hydraulic system of the tractor, controlled by an up-or-down handle below the side of the driver's seat. The wagon was a flatbed, with the exception of an upright board panel at the front, stabilized by a two-by-four A-frame that protruded a few feet above the board panel. The grain sheaves were stacked to within a few feet of the top of the A-frame. Dad's objective was to back the wagon into the garage, raise it with the hydraulic, place an old barrel under the tongue of the wagon, lower it onto the barrel, and unhook the tractor for another use.

Dad was likely cognizant of our arrival home, but he had his mind on his task and did not notice as I scampered into the garage, climbed up the back of the wagon onto the top of the sheaves, and worked my way to the front. As any boy might do, I held onto the A-frame and even opened my mouth and sort of bit down on the top of it as I looked down at Dad, who was in turn looking downward at the wagon tongue. Once he got the wagon to the desired location, he motioned to my brother to prepare to slide the barrel under the tongue so it could be unhooked. Just as Dad and my brother were oblivious to my presence on the wagon, so was I oblivious to the beam of the garage now positioned just inches above the back of my head. That is when it happened—"the scream heard around the town!" As the wagon rose upward, my head was for a very brief instant pinned between the A-Frame and the garage beam.

I was rushed back to Doc Madsen with blood streaming from my mouth. Was there an ambulance in town? Likely not in that day, but if so, my folks were not waiting around. I think Doc kidded me about not coming to see him at all since he delivered me, and now I was coming twice in one day. The A-frame had pushed my teeth around—my top teeth now closed behind the bottom teeth. The beam had slightly bruised the back of my head. Other than that, I was fine. I went back to my adventures.

It took a few years and several experiments to get my teeth straightened out. One idea was to have me lie flat on my back for an hour each day with my top teeth attached to a rubber band device hooked to the ceiling. We should have known that this would not work—Charlie had a standing offer to pay me fifty cents to sit still and quiet for five minutes and I could never seem to do it. Finally, a dentist constructed some type of a plate that covered my bottom teeth so that my downward bite forced my top teeth into position. There were some advantages—for a while, I even got to scamper down to Floyd's Drug Store during school lunch for a malt, as I could not chew whatever the school had to offer.

So life went on and I did not think much about my accident until an occasion when I was older and Dad recounted the frightening time. He told me of what he called my "blood-curdling scream heard all over town" but also, with his wry smile, reminded me that we lived in a small town. Then he analyzed the logic for me—had he waited *until* he heard me scream, it would have been too late. Human reaction time would not have sufficed for the quick action needed to drop the handle of the hydraulic and reverse the upward movement of the wagon. He said that before he ever heard me scream, he experienced a voice, or a force, or an impression—I am not exactly sure what he heard or felt— that he was to drop the hand that controlled the handle. Or perhaps his hand just dropped without any conscious forethought. I just know that it happened.

In my teaching through the years, I have shared this story many times with my students, exercising caution to teach that most spiritual manifestations are not usually dramatic. But I have tried to also teach them that the power and protection of the Holy Ghost can be "faster than a speeding bullet" when necessary. And for that, I am alive—and very grateful.

Chapter Nine:

Dennis the Menace and His Protégé

I grew up with television. We did not have a TV in our home when I was born, nor did many others of my generation. I was four or five when we got our first set and remember the excitement I felt when we purchased it from Golden Sanderson's Fairview Mercantile ("The Merc").

Viewing the *Lawrence Welk Show* became a Saturday night ritual for my parents—and is such still for Aunt Irene, age ninety-four, who lives with us here in Waunakee. I confess that I sometimes tune in with her—not so much from desire for the music or entertainment, but in pure nostalgia of the happy times in my home that we spent huddled around our TV. We loved *Walt Disney's Wonderful World of Color* and would dash home from Sunday worship to delight in its exciting and exotic adventures. The TV programming was mostly good, as I recall, and modeled honesty; courtesy; respect for others, for country, and for principles of right and wrong. My sister and I would draw along with John Gnagy by sticking a plastic sheet over the front of the screen and drawing on it as directed by the artist. We were entertained and uplifted by watching such classics as *Leave it to Beaver, Father Knows Best, My Three Sons, Zorro, Roy Rogers, Gomer Pyle, Lassie,* and *Daniel Boone.*

Few would argue that with the advent of television came a major shift in the mores of society. Many, however, debate the cause-and-effect relationship between the two. I know that I was changed by this new adventure into the world beyond Fairview. So were my Turpin cousins on the dairy, as they sometimes delayed the evening milking to view their favorite programs. But Uncle Clarence, who worked at the coal mine in his steel-toed boots, put all things right. One evening after his third trip into the house to retrieve the boys, he walked directly to the TV and furiously kicked one foot completely through the picture tube with the animated declaration, "Now maybe we will get the chores done!" It was years before they got another TV.

The influence of that *Dennis the Menace*[13] guy was the inception of my path to destruction. I suppose I could even be considered his protégé.

Dennis was not really a bad boy—just kind of clumsy and accident-prone. He was curious about things—particularly the activities of Mr. Wilson, his gruff old neighbor. Dennis did not always think through the long-term consequences of his antics as much as his parents and Mr. Wilson thought he should. But his saving grace was Mrs. Wilson, who adored Dennis and pretty much protected him from the exasperations of her husband. I felt a kindred spirit with Dennis.[14]

My delinquencies were small in the beginning. When I was at a Cub Scout meeting at the home of our den leader, Edith Cox, an outside cat put its face against the window pane, so I slipped over with some sort of marker and painted a nice big moustache on the cat and thereby succeeded in effecting the giggles of the group. I think by the time Edith caught on, the cat had departed, leaving the stand-alone mysterious moustache on the window.

En route to a family reunion in Sunnyside, we took a bit of a detour to the dynamite plant to procure some explosives for a stubborn rock at the farm. Dad placed the dynamite in the trunk of the car and we went on our way. When we entered the old highway tunnel at Castle Gate, I figured it would be a great moment to fire several shots from my new cap gun, which I did out of my open window. The echo of the tunnel amplified the noise and Dad panicked, thinking for a moment that the dynamite was exploding. We were lucky that in his terror, he was able to keep control of the car. I recall him using his oft-repeated trademark phrase, "That's when all hell broke loose," as he told the story at the reunion.

I really liked Pam, who was a few years younger than me. I plotted for days how I could show my interest in her but came up blank. I would like to think that when I did act, it was from impulse and not from deep character. As she walked from school, I ran over to her, stole her mittens, and wiped them in the waste oil of the old concrete grease-trap on the side of Mack's Garage. I was dismayed and confused that she did not appreciate my gesture. After my conscience taught me of my error, I felt guilty about it for years—deep down I knew I should apologize, but I never did. Never, that is, until this year! I attended church in Fairview and Pam's husband, Mike, taught the Sunday School lesson and shared his appreciation for his wife and how "kind and forgiving" she is. That gave me the needed courage, so I talked to her after class and apologized. She could not remember the incident, but laughed and said, "I forgive you." So Mike was right about her.

My Salt Lake cousins also contributed somewhat to my misbehavior. We pulled the common juvenile telephone pranks of calling people and asking, "Is Mr. Wall there? Mrs. Wall? Any Walls?" with the punch line, "Well then, how do you hold up your house?" and "Is there a road running past your house?" with the punch line, "You had better go catch it." I suppose these were mostly harmless pranks, albeit annoying to those we called. I am afraid we did throw a few eggs in our nighttime forays, and we also stole a few peas from Allie Carlson's garden next door to Grandma and Grandpa's place. I felt that I later redeemed myself when I hitched a ride home from Fairview Lakes with him during a rainstorm. I helped him load his little row boat and then, when his car got "stuck" in a huge mud puddle in the road and he was frantically revving his engine to no avail, I rescued us by suggesting that he move the gear shift from "neutral" to "drive."

We once stole Clair's bullwhip, took it to Grandpa's, climbed the tree with it, and then dangled it down in front of Clair as he trekked home. Shame on us! Once—or maybe twice—we discovered that we could sneak over to the old-time pop machine at the Skyline Motel and with a bottle opener, remove the cap from a bottle suspended vertically in the display racks and drink the contents with a straw without paying our dime. My older cousin Larry, whose parents owned the motel, avenged this wrong when he and his friends hung me by my pant cuffs on his picket fence and left me for the vultures. I do not remember who rescued me—just that I could not figure it out for myself without removing my pants, and I was far too shy for that.

Of my own volition as a menace, I threw the wires from my newspaper bundles into the leafy tree tops behind the post office. In the fall, when the trees were bare, my crime was exposed. One day after school hours, I broke into the school through a window (although I technically did not break anything, as the window had been left ajar) and retrieved my toy robot so I could take it to Grandma's and play with it as she tended me. From my perch high on the top of our loaded hay wagon, I once threw a dirt clod at a passing car, not realizing until after I released it that the driver-side window was open. The clod hit the passing businessman square in the chest and splattered his white shirt (fortunately the clod was dry). On another occasion, I splattered LeRoy's car with wet mud as he "dragged main" past our house. I have a fairly vivid memory of him stopping and pointing out to me the fancy bullwhip conveniently coiled on his back seat. I vowed then and there that I would never again throw mud specifically at him or at his car. It seems that I carried around a lot of guilty feelings as a young man.

My sister, Norma, was four years my senior and had friends her age through the block in three directions. I seemed drawn to the activities of this energetic and creative foursome—likely where I first acquired the title of "menace." I was frustrated that I was not always included in their adventures and that I could not understand their new language—Pig Latin, I think they called it—which I felt they had invented to exclude me.

Once when Norma was called to the phone, she asked if I would watch her cinnamon toast that she had just placed in the oven. "Sure," I replied. I pulled up a chair and watched it go from tan, to brown, to dark brown, to black, to flames. "But you only told me to watch it" was my defense.

Janet, the friend to the east, was assigned to help her father, Glen, operate the derrick system to hoist the hay into the barn. This derrick, mostly identical to the one we had in our barn, consisted of a steel track installed under the inside peak of the roof. A cable threaded on pulleys and gears spanned the distance. The hay wagon was parked on one end of the barn where a large set of steel "forks" were attached to the cable. The operator would set the forks into the hay and then lock them into position. The cable on the other side of the barn was hitched to a tractor or a horse. When the operator was ready for the hay to be hoisted, he would yell to the person on the other side to move the tractor or horse forward and lift the hay up into the desired position in the barn, and then the operator would pull a trip rope and release the hay. As it was difficult to hear from one end of the barn to the other, often a third person was stationed as a "relay" in view of both ends of the operation. This person would yell "ready" when it was time to lift the forks. I often worked as the relay and, when I got a bit older, as the tractor operator for our derrick system, so I was highly skilled at my craft. In retrospect, I should have just left it at that.

One day when Janet and her father were working the system without a relay, I hid myself in the bushes where I could see both parties and waited until just the right moment when the forks had been inserted into the hay, but not yet locked. I disguised my voice as best I could and yelled "ready," and then I watched as the horse pulled the empty forks up into the air, causing much frustration for Janet and her dad. I think I actually pulled this prank a few times over a few days until my older brother Ron got wind of it and then gave me a behind-the-barn scolding that I did not soon forget. In later years, I think my anger at Ron and my embarrassment for my action turned to gratitude that he had actually saved me from damnation or death.

But there seems to be a strange irony in all things—Ron himself was often more menace than angel. I best not go too far astray in detailing his exploits, or I would need to write another book, but I will just offer one example. He and his friends would fish the San Pitch at the "posted" portion on Heber's property during the time they knew he would be in sacrament meeting. One day, Heber surprised them and caught them in the act. He preached them a fiery sermon they did not soon forget—that is, except for Cousin Reid, who chose to remain in hiding seated on a red-ant bed in the willows rather than emerge and face the rebuke of the patriarch.

Norma once invited Peggy, a college friend, to visit for the weekend. I knew that Peggy had dated George from Fairview, and I was not sure if they had broken up or if the relationship was just inactive or what the situation was. But as I eavesdropped on the girl talk, I felt a strange compulsion to try my hand at matchmaking. At church, I told George that I thought Peggy really liked him. Later at home, I told Peggy that George really liked her. Sometime later, they married and since they are still married and living in Fairview at present after all these years, I take full credit for it, even though I am honestly not sure my actions had anything to do with it. But at least there was an element of pure motive in this round of mischief.

Dad even contributed to my wandering ways when he taught me as a not-yet-sixteen–year-old to drive on Sunday mornings as we delivered newspapers on the canyon road and then to the end of Milburn Road. I loved these adventures! One morning, I was going too fast for the loose gravel on the shoulder of the road and knocked Fred Mower's mailbox—pole and all—clear into his front yard. I learned the art of "dog rolling"—as a dog chased the car, I would unlatch the door and wait for just the right moment when it was running close and parallel and then open the door wide and fast (In retrospect, I sincerely hope I did not cause any harm. I think my rearview mirror view of the startled dogs always showed them standing and shaking off the dust).

Dean was a customer on our Sunday route who lived with his wife in an old trailer house amidst the junkyard he operated. Their home, inside and out, was well guarded by what seemed like no less than a hundred mean dogs—but I think the actual count was only thirteen (If I am not mistaken, I think this was the setting in world history of the invention of the term "meaner than a junkyard dog"). The property could not have been in more disrepair. I marveled when Uncle Jack went to Provo to visit Dean during a hospital stay and came home and reported that he had said, "I need to get home—you know, when you leave a place, it really goes to hell." It already seemed to have gone there to me, and I was terrified to try to get to the house to collect my due. I asked him if he would bring the money to our house each month. He did, and would stand just inside the kitchen door and talk to my mother for what seemed like forever. I soon concocted a fake phone call scheme of causing the phone to ring and then announcing to my mother that she was wanted on a call. I do not recall that she ever scolded me for my deceit by thus rescuing her.

One day, Uncle Keith sent me to Price to deliver a load of newly sawn lumber. We loaded it on the flatbed truck and measured the overhang off the back to be just less than four feet so we did not have to install the red flag required by law for overhangs of over four feet. At the Soldier Summit weigh station, the officer motioned me over and came out of the office with a tape measure in his hand saying that he wanted to measure the load. I was not at all worried until I exited the truck and noticed that the load had shifted backward a bit in the ascent up the canyon. As quick as a flash, my naturally helpful nature engaged and I jumped to the aid of the officer, offering to hold one end of the tape. I quickly turned this one-handed task into a two-handed task, hiding both hands under the planks with one hand holding the end of the tape measure against the truck bed. Then before the officer could stretch out the tape, I casually transferred the tape end to the other hand held several inches away from the truck bed. "Hmm, I thought for sure your overhang was more than four feet," he said as he sent me on my way. Whew!

Was this clever? Yes. Was it honest? No. Did I care? Not then. Did I care later? Yes. Do I care now? Well, let's just say that it was an event of long ago and that it was soon time for me to graduate high school, join the army, and go on a mission, where my downward spiral of mischief was thwarted somewhat as I was taught discipline and love of country. My youthful days as a first-class menace are now long behind me and on a good day, I think my wife might even concede that I am probably not nearly the troublemaker that I once was

Chapter Ten

Tell My Mother I Am OK

In Fairview, we may have been sheltered from smog but not from tragedy and sorrow. People lived serious lives of hard work, failure, success, trial, and heartache. And yet we seemed to find pleasure and deep satisfaction in simple things—growing a garden, mowing the lawn, and painting the house.

Blaine and Lucile were such people. They were our adjoining neighbors to the northeast. Glen and Paul were their oldest children and were close to the age of my older siblings. Although their two youngest children, Debra and Leon, were younger than I was, we were childhood playmates. I spent many hours with them in their big, old two-story house or exploring the neighborhood. I remember Lucile as outgoing and happy. She worked hard and kept their home spotlessly clean. She was jovial and witty. Blaine seemed more reserved. He was always working and seemed to be the epitome of thrift and self-reliance. I recall how he salvaged discarded wooden pallets from his job at the turkey plant and built a sturdy work shed at the foot of their garden. Lucile was an "Avon Lady" for more than two decades. Together, they kept that huge garden as clean and beautiful as the rest of the property. Lucile took great pride in her blue ribbon tomatoes. I remember how Blaine would spend hours on a high ladder meticulously painting the frame house white with black trim. They loved hunting, fishing, and camping.

To supplement income and provide work opportunities for the children, they harvested night crawlers and sold them to fishermen who followed a sign placed on Main Street at the corner of our pasture. I recall a conversation once when Lucile was asked what her husband did in church. With that perpetual twinkle in her eye, she replied, "Oh, he spends hours at church gathering night crawlers from the lawn." I competed with them for a few years, but their worms always seemed healthier and better managed than my own. During the summer of 1957, Glen harvested and sold enough night crawlers to buy his own school clothes, proudly worn at North Sanpete Junior High School in Moroni.

The two large chestnut trees in their front yard were a source of much fascination to me. They were beautiful in their foliage and bloom. When the nuts were in the "spiked" phase, we picked them and used them for weapons in our neighborhood boy wars. Once the spiked shell peeled off, we used the brown nuts for a sort of crude game of marbles, strung them together as necklaces, or loaded them as exotic cargo on our toy trucks and trains. Sometimes the joy came in seeing how many nuts I could collect—a flour sack full was a real treasure. I do not remember ever trying to roast them "on an open fire" as the Christmas song goes, but we may have done. I notice that the home and the two chestnut trees are still standing today.

Sunday, October 6, 1957, is a day that burns vividly in my mind, although I did not personally experience very much of the sad events of the day. I was only six and was kept at home. We had just returned from church and I remember following my mother to our back door as she ran to answer the frantic pounding and shouting. Paul was there with the panicked declaration, "Glen has hung himself and we can't find Debra." Glen was tending Debra and they were the only ones home. Paul had arrived to find the tragedy. Leon had not yet been born. The event was clearly determined to be accidental. I doubt anyone knows the exact details, as Debra was only three years old, but as I recall, they had been playing on a tire swing hanging from one of the chestnut trees and Glen had somehow gotten his neck caught in the rope and fallen. My sister, Norma, followed my mother to scene and discovered that little Debra had gone into the house and fallen asleep under a bed.

I am sure Blaine and Lucile were heartbroken. As this was well before the time of my childhood friendship with Debra and Leon, I have no memory of interacting much with the family then. I just know that it was tough and that the Stevens family must have suffered the remorse familiar to anyone who goes through such a horrific trial. "Why?" and "What could we have done?" were undoubtedly their troubling questions during their time of heartache and trial.

Several months ago, I was wandering the Fairview Cemetery, keeping notes and seeking memory prompts, when I paused at the graves of Albert and Lillian Hansen, parents of my sister-in-law Louise. Nearby, I had just paused at Glen's grave and recalled his tragic death and my acquaintance with his family. I called Louise in Idaho to say hello and to tell her that I was standing at her parents' graves. When I mentioned that I was also near Glen's grave, I asked if she remembered him and how close they were in age. She said she knew him well and that they were the same age. Then she told me a story I had never heard before.

Louise was ill and regretted being unable to attend Glen's funeral. They were junior high classmates. About a week after Glen's death and funeral, Louise and her friend were walking to their home economics class in the two-story white building adjacent to the main school building. The band room was on the bottom floor, with home economics on the upper floor. As they turned toward the stairwell to go up, they glanced through the open classroom door and looked into the band room. There was Glen, dressed in his new blue jeans and red plaid shirt. He was putting his horn in its case and looked up at Louise and her friend and said, "Tell my mother I am OK." Then he was gone. As Louise and her friend continued up the stairs, she turned to her friend and queried, "Did you see what I just saw?" and the friend described an identical scene to what Louise had experienced. Within a few days, Louise went to Lucile and delivered the welcome message from her departed son.[15]

I have never had such a personal experience—never seen an angel or a departed spirit. To my knowledge, I have never heard a voice from beyond the grave or even felt the close proximity of a departed loved one. I am curious about such things as how they could be dressed in their mortal appearance and why they appear to some and not others. I do not know. I am patient and assured that we will know some day. But, because of my theology and belief in life after death, I do not doubt the sincere stories of honest and humble people. And I am happy that Glen is OK.

Chapter Eleven:

The Sidekick

Dad was an entertainer. I did not inherit his musical ability or his flair for acting, although I have spent my life presenting to folks in a different way. My first memory of Dad's stage persona was of him as our ward's Santa. Some of the happiest memories of my young life were of our ward Christmas socials in the cultural hall of the Fairview South Ward. We had songs, skits, games, and a delightful bag of nuts and homemade candy given to each child as we sat on the lap of a jolly and animated old Santa who seemed remarkably familiar to me. When I did dash home once after the program to discover Dad removing his white beard, I was heartbroken. Norma recalls that I wailed for a good long time as this unwelcome truth settled in.

The headline of a 1970 edition of the *Mt. Pleasant Pyramid* reads, "Unique Fairview Band Boasts of Forty-Two Years Playing Together" ("Playing together" may have been a loose interpretation of their harmony, but perhaps only according to my untrained ear). A line in the article reads, "The baby of the group is Buford 'Boots' Christensen, who plays the accordion." He was fifty-seven at the time and was indeed the youngest member. Spud Anderson provided the bass with his genuine GI gas can and wooden shovel handle strung with a nylon cord. Fred Gardner, then eighty-one, played the guitar, the triangle, and an authentic washboard, which he strummed with sewing thimbles. His wife, Sarah, played the harmonica. Lyndon Graham expanded his talents beyond his Indian lore and artifacts and carving to playing the steel guitar and the mandolin. Alta Osborne performed the piano accompaniment.

This group met on Monday nights for FHE and practice (Folks did not worry much about separation of church and state or culture in Fairview in those days—all band members were Mormons, so a spiritual thought from the prophet blended well with *Roses of Picardy*). When the practice was held at our home, I was doubly thrilled by the aura of the band, with their unique and fun personalities, and my mother's signature cream puffs, ice cream, and chocolate sauce—all homemade. They sometimes debated among themselves as to whether the practice sessions helped or not, but concluded at least they were no worse than they were last month, "so let's keep at it." They were constantly adjusting their playlist to include such varied favorites as, "Golden Slippers," "Somewhere My Love," "When It's Springtime in the Rockies," and some novelty songs such as "Who Threw the Overalls in Mrs. Murphy's Chowder?" and "How Much Is That Doggie in the Window?" I well remember when they shook the very spiritual foundations of the community by adding "Itsy Bitsy Teenie Weenie Yellow Polka Dot Bikini" to the playlist. Some were sure they would be run out of town with tar and feathers, but folks generally seemed to like it. It was all for fun.

The Harmonica Band performed for nursing homes, weddings, and missionary and servicemen farewells. Dad even constructed an old-time horse-drawn band wagon to haul the band in parades and special events. On one later occasion, when I was in the bishopric and we held our ward campout on our farm property, we loaded a piano from the school on a flatbed wagon, rounded up the band members as best we could, and had them perform at our evening campfire. The old folks talked about it for years (And they are likely talking about it still in their heavenly realm).

The band's capstone performance came when they were invited to perform one Sunday afternoon on Eugene Jelesnik's *Talent Showcase* TV program in Salt Lake City. The whole town talked for days before and after about this new-found notoriety. I had a bit of fun with my response. When someone asked, "What did you think of the TV appearance?" I replied, "Oh, I thought it was great! The best part about them being on TV was that I could turn it off whenever I wanted."

For several years, Dad and a few of the band members teamed up with others in town for a three-night annual production of an old-time minstrel show. This may seem a strange thing for an all-white Western community to do—especially during the changing world of civil rights—but I am confident they would certainly not do so in today's climate. Events such as the murder of Emmett Till, Dr. King's march on Washington, the Montgomery bus boycott sparked by Rosa Parks, and LBJ's Civil Rights Act were, for me, just newsprint headlines. It would yet be a decade or so before I would receive my first experience with African American culture in army basic training. It would be two decades before I would read Alex Haley's *Roots: The Saga of an American Family* and receive my first real exposure to the ugly horrors of the cancer of slavery that had so polluted and sickened our nation.[16]

The main memories I have of the shows are that old Frank Larsen was the tap dancer, Grandpa Tucker was one of the star musicians with his voice and guitar, Dad was the prominent comic, and I was his sidekick.[17] Each year, Dad thought long and hard about his next gimmick. One year, his routine was about one of the troupe who had died and, as they had all assumed, gone to heaven. We took lumber and some old speakers and metal parts and constructed what Dad called "his newfangled wireless telephone." When he bragged to the others that his new contraption would let him call farther than they had ever thought possible, one of the guys suggested that they try to contact their dearly departed friend, who was surely to be found at the pearly gates. Dad said that would for sure work, and it did—he connected with Saint Peter. The problem was their departed friend was not there. After looking for him, word came back that perhaps they would have more success by calling down under—not Australia. There was a long, tense moment waiting for the call to Hades to connect. When it did, in Dad's trademark expression, "all hell broke loose" as I passed a signal to Ron, who was in our parked car just outside the stage door. He started the engine and thus detonated several "car bombs" attached to Dad's telephone (not to be confused with the Irish cocktail or modes of modern terrorism). These bombs might be described as super fire-crackers on steroids that were wired to the car so they would detonate when the engine started. They were quite harmless if one kept a reasonable distance from them—there was no shrapnel or poison. We created some extra smoke to coincide with the car bombs. The point was made that the departed friend had gone below and it was not to be a pleasant conversation.

I do not recall the exact plot involved in us turning a live badger loose in the audience, but that is what we did, to the fright and consternation of all patrons. Along with Fred Gardner, we had constructed a wooden box with a spring-loaded door on the front. We made sure that the audience understood that we had a live badger in the box, but we did not give them a hint of anticipation that we were actually going to turn it loose. At the appropriate punch line, the latch was activated and the door snapped open. People clambered in all directions to escape the angry badger as it ran through the hall. I also do not recall the breed of Fred's pet dog, but we had determined that it was of appropriate size and shape to pass for a badger if we painted it with some striping and marking. The ruse did not hold for long, but long enough to give the folks a good fright.

The badger-in-the-audience routine inspired my favorite performance the following year—my favorite because I was able to play a more involved and critical role. The ploy involved baking an elaborate cake to celebrate a birthday for one of the company. Dad and I constructed a fairly large "cook stove" out of lumber, complete with oven, top burners, and a metal stove pipe. We made plenty of room for me and a lot of stuff to hide inside the stove. We then constructed a large round baking pan for the cake, including a false lid with a concealed compartment. In the routine, Dad hammed up the baking of the cake, assuring one and all that this was to be the most "unique cake they had ever seen" (He got that right). He poured and mixed the ingredients and then placed it in the oven, which soon began to smoke with a bit of help from the sidekick. This was indeed tragic—the cake could be ruined.

Someone suggested that the stovepipe may be plugged, so Dad reached his hand down inside to see what he could find. One of my duties from my concealed place inside the stove was to hand the items up to Dad through the pipe (We rehearsed this several times). Sure enough, he began to extract one thing after another—an umbrella, a top hat, a toilet plunger, a ball, and an old-fashioned women's corset girdle. Dad had a way of eliciting laughter from the audience with each new item. Finally, it was suggested that he should remove the stovepipe for further inspection. As he did so, he unveiled a beautiful bouquet of flowers, the final item that I had placed inside the pipe, supported underneath by a trap door I closed to hold the vase.

With the flowers set aside and the stovepipe reinstalled, Dad offered assurance that he could now bake the cake. During the process of cleaning out the stovepipe, I had exchanged the actual baking pan holding the mixed ingredients with the identical-looking trick one with the false lid, within which we had concealed our surprise. Finally, the great moment came when the cake was baked and the pan was set in plain sight for all to see. Dad encouraged the excitement to the great anticipation of all of the players and audience. Then at last, at the climax, Dad lifted the lid, freeing the false compartment in the process. As everyone watched in wondered eagerness, two live magpies tethered together by a long piece of fish line escaped the cake tin and flew into the audience, squawking and flapping and exciting the frantic pandemonium of people scattering in all directions.

For this, as with all of the performances, Dad, his sidekick, and his friends felt that we had at least given the guests their money's worth of memorable excitement.

Chapter Twelve:

The Curator, the Coach, and the Telephone Man

Had someone asked me five years or so ago how many people I knew who had positively influenced my life, I would have perhaps said, "Oh, maybe a few hundred." Today, I would say, "Thousands and counting." Facebook is a part of my perception change—I have had an incredibly gratifying experience the past few years connecting with long-time friends, relatives, and former students and colleagues. As I interact with these folks, I realize how so many people have been such a positive part of my life. One of the sweetest truths I have ever learned is that of a lasting "sociality" that exists in the eternal realm.[18]

As I was considering how to convey a glimpse of people who have made my life better, I thought that there would not be enough space in any book or memoir to do so justly, even if I restricted my thoughts only to those with Fairview ties. If I expanded my view to Sanpete County or to other places I have lived, it would be nearly impossible to even try to list them—let alone pay my desired tribute. I decided to choose three men from my youth, Golden Sanderson, Jerry Nelson, and Iven Cox, as a representative sampling of the whole and offer a brief description of them and their lives and service.

About the time I was considering this approach, my friend Ed Cox gave a profound talk at the commencement exercises of the Snow College-Richfield campus. I have communicated with him about the talk and he has graciously shared a complete transcript with me and given his permission for me to reference it. He told of two men who were already on my short list, and from his tribute to them, I realized how much they had also influenced my own life.

The Curator

I did not personally know Golden Sanderson as well as the other two men, but I vividly remember his tireless work and effort to meet the needs of Fairview residents as manager of the Fairview Merc. As this was the store nearest my home, I frequented it often. The sights and smells of the Merc were always fascinating and exciting to me. Sometimes I followed Golden into the store rooms and got a glimpse of behind-the-scenes efforts. I marveled at how he could keep everything so well organized and displayed. Golden loved to tell of the Merc and how "you could buy anything there from a threshing machine to a paper of pins in the old days."[19] I remember Golden as quick-witted, jolly, and full of energy—ready to tackle whatever challenge faced him. One day he even peaceably settled an on-site dispute over a candy bar my sister and I had purchased in his store.

I do not know if Golden has ever been officially known as the "Father of the Fairview Museum," but to me, he certainly was. For many years, Golden was the energy and vision of the museum. Dad served on the board in the early days and most of my association with Golden came as Dad and I worked with him on museum business.

Golden had his heroes—two of the greatest being Celestia and Peter Peterson. This fine couple may well hold the distinction of being the world's longest married couple. After the Guinness World Records organization bestowed this honor upon a couple from Great Britain, a Peterson grandson worked to set the record straight. In a *Deseret News* article, Lee Benson wrote, "According to Reed Madsen of Richfield, his grandparents, the late Peter and Celestia Peterson of Fairview, are the true world champions of marriage. Peter and Celestia were married 81 years, 10 months, and 320 days when Peter died 45 years ago at the age of 100 on Oct. 27, 1960. Celestia died a year later at the age of 101. The Petersons were married in St. George on Dec. 11, 1878, when they were both 18."[20]

Reed continues, "In Fairview, the Petersons are a household name. When Peter and Celestia were still alive, they were the talk of the town. On their 75th wedding anniversary there was a town day just for them. On their 80th anniversary, telegrams and congratulations came from everywhere, including President Eisenhower. . . . What I remember most is when they were older and them sitting in their kitchen in their matching rockers with their feet up on the oven door."[21] I remember visiting the Petersons with Dad. Perhaps they had their feet on the oven door then.

As thirty years of business at the Merc began to wind down, Golden focused his energy more to the inception of the Fairview Museum. He helped orchestrate the talents of renowned sculptor Avard Fairbanks to portray a monument to Peter and Celestia Peterson. Mr. Fairbanks actually purchased the old school in the beginning, but it was

Golden and Lyndon Graham who finally took over the management, formed a non-profit corporation, and went to work procuring funds to further the cause of the museum. Golden's passion for this project led to the museum being declared a "national shrine to love and devotion" in honor of the Petersons.

Golden seemed tireless in finding and collecting historic treasures from far and wide. He began filling the rooms and halls of the old school with artifacts of farming, fishing, mining, and millwork. His cheery but determined personality elicited confidence in folks who willingly dusted off their historic treasures and entrusted them to the growing museum. One of his greatest accomplishments was bringing the lifetime artistry and Indian relics of his friend Lyndon Graham to public display for all to enjoy. As the interior of the building began to fill, work was begun on the exterior with the procurement of old farm implements, steam engines, antique construction equipment, and an array of old buggies and wagons. Dad donated one of his restored buggies for display. My proximity to the liveliness inspired me to donate my junior high woodshop project, a glass showcase, for use in the museum (This was a small contribution, I know, but I was a small boy caught up in the energy of the pursuit. For me, it was significant that I could add to the effort).

Golden was a marvelous man who inspired goodness in others and helped unveil the rich, historic past of the dedicated souls who struggled so hard to live well in this beautiful place. I am grateful to have been a personal witness to his worthy cause.

The Coach

Many times I watched in awe as Jerry Nelson, with his one good arm, caught a baseball in his mitt, flipped both mitt and ball into the air, caught only the ball as the mitt fell to the ground, and then threw the ball straight as an arrow to his desired target—and all of that so fast that it seemed if you blinked, you would miss it. I have also watched him hold a ball and bat in his hand, toss the ball into the air and then place-hit it with a speed and accuracy that put us young admirers to shame.

Ed Cox described Jerry's early accident in his commencement address at Snow College:

Jerry Nelson was ten years old in the summer of 1942. He had gone with his father from Fairview to Scofield to spend the week to help in a new coal mine that his uncle and several men from

Fairview were mining. Jerry helped dump the coal from the coal cars that the horses pulled out of the mine to the tipple. He was standing on a four-foot square platform thirty feet in the air when some of the coal from the coal car went the wrong way and hit the platform. This would be the last time Jerry would feel or use his left arm in this life. Jerry stepped back and plunged head first on to steel rails some thirty feet below. He landed on his left shoulder, causing all the nerve endings in the left side of his upper torso to be torn from his spine. Years later he would learn that the fall had also broken his neck.[22]

From my limited observation, Jerry seemed to live life as though his accident had not happened. Oh, I am sure there were countless things he struggled to do, and undoubtedly he experienced frustration and discouragement, but he lived life. He worked hard, got a good education, married well, reared a good family, bought and maintained a home and yard, and served in church and community.

He rounded up the boys of my age in town and those just younger and just older and organized us into Fairview's first little league baseball team. He elicited parental support for transportation and community support for funding to purchase uniforms, which we proudly wore. My fancy cap with the big, bold *F* on the front became a permanent part of me. I was proud to explain to folks from far and wide that the *F* was for Fairview—a great little town—and that I was a member of its finest baseball team (I withheld the fact that we were the only team). Within just a few years, Jerry took our evolving little team to compete in the state championship tournament in Orem.

I was personally not very good and have never seemed to have much aptitude for athletics, but Jerry did not seem to care—he made me feel important and encouraged me at every turn. The highlight of my career came when I was at bat in the regional Lion's Club tournament at Snow College and solidly connected with a strong pitch. I gaped in disbelief with flashes of glory streaming my mind as the ball soared high into the air headed for the turf behind the centerfield fence—and then hit the fence just a few inches short of the top and landed in the outfield. It seemed that folks were wild with their cheers and congratulations, but Jerry stayed calm and called out to me that it might be a good idea to break out of my trance and make a dash for first base—which I did, just barely avoiding an out. As I caught my breath on first, over the loudspeaker came the sweet announcement of my name and an award of a free root beer from the Ephraim A&W for my hit! My sports career never got any better than that—and did not need to. I had relished my moment of fame.

Jerry was an educator by "precept and example," as our old saying went. He taught at the junior high school in Moroni when I attended there and offered a sense of connection and well-being through this challenging time of my life. It was good to know he was there—to receive his warm smile and his personable and encouraging support. Many years later, we inadvertently met him in an airport of a distant city as he was traveling to an education conference. Our meeting brought a flood of good and grateful memories as I proudly introduced him to my wife.

Jerry was an entrepreneur. He and his wife, Lavon, were visionaries. They developed and constructed the first and only ski resort in our area, the Snowland Ski Area, to include a lodge, a lift, and a downhill run. By now, our little league days were behind us, but I skied at Snowland and occasioned visits to the lodge as a warming break from snowmobile outings.

So how do I honor this great man who gave so much to me and to so many? At this moment, on a snowy February morning in Wisconsin, I have been frustrated for days about an assignment I have. It seems that my best efforts are falling short of the success I desire. I have considered resigning. But in my mind's eye, I think of the occasion fifty years ago when Jerry reminded me to pull out of my trance and make a run for it. I think that I will.

The Telephone Man

As a teenager, one evening I was witness to a fascinating clash of cultures. The occasion was a summer outdoor high priest social around the campfire at the Wagon Wheel Campground. The menu was mutton and sourdough. It was prepared by our neighbor Ross Johnson who had perfected his art through his many years as a sheepherder. The entertainment was a fledgling local rock band headed up by Branch Cox. The volume was loud. The "agent" who had somehow booked the show into this incongruous venue was Iven Cox. Some of the old folks offered up an amusing charade by holding their hands over their ears during the performance. Undoubtedly, some likely considered that the Fairview Harmonica Band would have been a more appropriate fit for the occasion.

To me at the time, Iven seemed oblivious to the culture clash. He just proceeded, in his characteristic passion, to introduce and laud the band. I am confident that I did not get it then, but I get it now—Iven championed people (In this case, it was his son). He was willing to assume risk and was not deterred by criticism. He just plowed forward in bettering the people of Fairview and the worthy causes of our community.

I turn to Ed's talk again to convey a significant reference point in the life of Iven Cox:

> My Uncle Iven was a telephone man. At age twenty-four he was in the prime of his life. It was the fall of 1939. An early snowstorm had taken down an open wire telephone line that served our little community. He had climbed a pole to untangle the shorted line when it came in contact with a 2200-volt power line.
>
> Witnesses say he was thrown from the pole like a rag doll, his hair and clothing a ball of fire. The jolt when he hit the ground was so hard that it probably started his heart beating again. Because there was no hospital in Fairview, he was taken to Doc. Sam Rigby's home, where for weeks the good doctor's wife cared for him in a back bedroom. Dr. Sam amputated his right arm and cut off two fingers on his left hand. Miraculously, he did not die.[23]

Iven, like Jerry, lived life. We grew comfortable with his "handicaps"—probably because I never recall him showing us any hint that he was handicapped. With his gloved prosthetic arm and the remaining fingers of his left hand, he continued his trade, adapting his new physique to the tasks at hand. I recall being fascinated as he gave us a tour of his switchboard and explained how our telephone calls were transmitted. He cared about people and worked hard to bring them the best possible service. One example of his extra-mile service was when he configured a special line from the South Ward church building to the home of the aged Peter and Celestia Peterson in their homebound days so they could listen to sacrament meetings. That was Iven—always helping in whatever way he could.

One winter morning, Iven and Dad teamed up to give our scout troop a sledding party we would never forget. In those days, the Fairview Canyon road was not plowed through in the winter time, but the first mile or so was occasionally plowed, providing a nice bank of snow as a sort of a safety rail on the canyon side of the road and a clear sledding run on the snow-packed road free of traffic. Dad parked his old sheep camp at the bottom of the run, stoked a warm fire and filled us up with all of the hot chocolate and sourdough pancakes we could eat.

I wonder if perhaps when you have so closely cheated death as Iven had done, you become more daring. That seemed the case that day. Iven tied a long rope to his old station wagon and at the end of the rope secured an old-fashioned bull-nosed car hood. We could tie our sleds to the rope for a tow up the hill, or just ride in the inverted car hood. Once everyone was on board, Iven would take off for the top like "a bat out of hell," as Dad described such things. The boys who were not going to sled down the canyon would pile back into the car hood for the downhill ride. Never before or since have I experienced a sledding adventure quite like this one. The ascent nearly matched the descent for speed and excitement.

The exhilarating climatic scene of the day for me was when, on Iven's downhill run, the car hood full of boys slipped into the ditch on the mountain side of the road and slid along for a while until the bullnose collided with the open end of a steel culvert, snapping the rope and instantly stopping the hood. The boys, of course, kept going for a fast skim along the surface of the snow. "Decapitation," although a very real possibility of this scenario, was not a vocabulary word on the tip of our tongues. Perhaps it was on Iven's, because this stunt did not receive a repeat performance.

Iven organized the first Cub Scout program in our community. Dedicated leaders were appointed and we entered a wonderful world of crafts, games, cooking, and skill development. I am not sure but would guess that Iven was perhaps the impetus for the exciting trip to the Salt Lake airport and the train ride back to Thistle that I have already described. In typical fashion, Iven demonstrated his unselfishness and commitment to the program by constructing what he called a "rumpus room" above his garage to be used for our pack meetings and other events. I still recall our first such meeting in the new rumpus room—I was in awe of a fascinating night of displaying and playing with our trains made from oatmeal boxes and from having a room designated just for us! I suppose we felt as special and as important as Cub Scouts anywhere could feel.

Iven's passion and love for life and service carried him squarely into the midst of myriad challenges to make the world a better place. He started the first credit union in Fairview. I am grateful that in my youth, I was witness to and recipient of his shared talents and selfless service. All the while, he plodded along in the care and keeping of his struggling little Fairview Telephone Company. As I have traveled the wandering roads of my life's quest, I have lost track of much of the ongoing saga of Fairview and have known little of Iven's legacy in the days since I have been gone. But now as I have been learning what the subsequent generations have done with the heritage—both in business and in service and family—bequeathed to them by Iven, I have developed a hunch. I believe that so much of the current success so apparent in the continuing legacy of service and caring is firmly rooted in the sublime principle that Iven Cox championed people.

Chapter Thirteen:
A Martyr for the Cause

I attended my kindergarten year in the old building that is now the Fairview Museum with Gladys Christensen as our teacher. The next year, the building was vacated and elementary students were all shifted just across the playground to the newer school that had been vacated by the junior high students, who were now being bused to Moroni. My first day of kindergarten was undoubtedly a traumatic day for my mother. I was her baby and I was recovering from my farming accident. Also, the story of her incessant weeping and wailing for many weeks on the occasion of when she started school in the same building was legendary in our family—she had been tightly bound to her mother's apron strings. But I think I did fine. My memories of kindergarten are mostly limited to playing leapfrog on the well-oiled hardwood floors in the downstairs halls, the nap/blanket/juice each day, and my perception that there were a bunch of scary big kids in the other rooms of the old school.

Our classes were small. An old photo shows twelve of us in first grade with Edda Graham as our teacher and Maitland Graham as our principal. I can name them all—the "North Warders" were LaMont Christensen, Penny Peckham, Kim Bench, Vangie Howell, David Fowles, Randy Nielsen, Karl Mower, and David Johnson. There were four South Warders—Karen Nielsen, Ed Cox, Kenneth Seeley, and myself. From second grade forward, we doubled our class size by combining with the group just older than us. Our teachers during these years were Winnie Rasmussen, Alice Stewart, Darrell Stewart, Leon Nielsen, and Mirth Miner, respectively.

One vivid memory I have from first grade was of a huge, elevated indoor sandbox at the side of our classroom. I went there to play one day and promptly demolished an abandoned sand castle to make room for my own project. I soon found myself being choked to death by a strong arm around my neck courtesy of the proprietor of the now-defunct sand castle. Just as I was taking my final gasp of breath, I did the only thing I could think to do—I stabbed my attacker in the leg with a pair of scissors

(This altercation likely prompted the invention of safety scissors for little kids). At this point, our teacher intervened and Karl, my assailant, was left to silently plot his revenge.

When the end-of-the-day bell rang, I gathered my things and exited the school in anticipation of a bee line to the safety of my home, only to be confronted by Karl. He had organized all of the other boys in the class as an execution squad to mete out my justice. I remember standing on the playground in fear and trembling as I faced a whole lineup of angry boys ready to beat me senseless. At what I was sure would be my final moment of life on this earth, someone in the line pointed out what was already particularly obvious to me—this would not be a fair fight. At that point, some of the boys were assigned to stand with me to offer a balance of power. The battle then turned into a rough and tumble of little boy games that soon ended without further incident, and I walked home grateful to live yet another day. But I was now battle-hardened, having faced death. I gained a degree of courage and confidence that would yet serve me well in just a few short years when I enlisted in the defense of my countrymen at the time of the great stink-base wars.

Our teachers were diligent, caring, and practical. I recall my excitement when Mr. Miner asked if anyone had a picture of a whale they could bring for show and tell. After school, I hurried home to our treasured volumes of the *Books of Knowledge* and, with my scissors, proudly sacrificed that page for the common and collective good of my school class. I was heartsick and embarrassed the next day when Mr. Miner clarified that he had said *quail* rather than *whale*.

I have pleasant memories of serving in the lunch room. I donned a crisp white apron and hat and served up the lunch fare for the day to my classmates, then scraped much of it into the slop barrels to be carted off to feed someone's pigs. I also loved bell-ringing duty because I could reach high and pull hard on the strong rope to swing the heavy cast iron bell, then jump upward as the rope retracted to give the sensation that I was flying. My goal was to ring it so hard that it would crack to rival that Liberty Bell we had learned about. I also gained satisfaction from creating a noise heard around the town.

Each year, we celebrated May Day. We danced in review for the parents and braided our intricate May Pole with our individual ribbons that our mothers had pressed to perfection. We also carried guns to school that day so we could soak each other's shirts—but when the principal caught us, he promptly confiscated them and smashed them under his heel.

One spring, LaMont and I spent our recess times huddled in a corner of the playground with writing tablets and pencils, intricately planning our great cowboy adventure. We were to take my Dad's sheep camp and horses and Lamont's horses and go off into the mountain wilderness where we would hunt and fish and live like mountain men. We could hardly wait for the last day of school. When it came, we each went about our summer activities without a second thought to our planned adventure. Since he lived in Indianola, we did not meet again until fall.

We sat in old wooden school desks. Two or three of them were fastened together on board runners so we could not wander them or lean them back. The desks were complete with ink wells, but we no longer used them by my time. Our teacher once disciplined a husky classmate by tying him to his desk with a strong rope. Once his desk set was vacated by the others, he stood up and walked off with it—but not too far, as it would not quite fit through the classroom door.

Often in our recess time, we played all sorts of games within the limits of our school rules. We generally disciplined each other for ill behavior—like when Ruth Ann threw me on the hardwood gym floor and bloodied my nose. After school hours, we played war games, organizing into neighborhood factions with forts of hay bales in our barns and wooden swords of our own making. With garbage can lids for shields, we collected and hurled spike-shelled chestnuts at each other. But all of this seemed mere training for the ultimate battle—stink base.

Stink base was a game of energy, strategy, and cooperation and was considered king of the old country school games. It consisted of two teams lined up on opposite ends of the playground. Players would run out of the safe zone of the home base and try to tag a member of the opposing team, thus designating him to the prisoner base, or the stink base. A person could only be tagged by someone who had departed his home base at a later moment than the one being pursued. As we had neither officials nor instant replay cameras, much of our time was spent arguing over who had first left home base. A prisoner could only be freed by one of his teammates infiltrating enemy territory to reach and tag him.

My primary memory of our stink base adventures was of Mr. Darrell Stewart, our fourth grade teacher. He played the game with us and offered a very unfair advantage to whichever team he chose to join. In my child's eye, he was a giant—plus he worked for the U.S. Forest Service in summertime, which, as far as I was concerned, put him right up there with Daniel Boone and Jim Bridger and made him a man not to be underestimated. He also once shot a bear, placing the capstone on his invincibility. He would win at stink base by the sheer force of his size and character—he would roar down the field with such strength and bellowing noise that no one ever seemed to even attempt to get near enough to tag him.

I do not know what came over me on that fateful day, but I made an inner, private decision that I was going to tag Mr. Stewart. I mustered my nerve, shelved my sanity, and charged straight at him. That is when the lights went out for me. I fell to the ground in a helpless coma. For what may well have been the only time in the history of Fairview Elementary school, Mr. Stewart was on stink base.

At this the game ended and Mr. Stewart picked me up, dusted me off and, to the praises of my teammates, tenderly escorted me back into the classroom. I felt rather dizzy for the rest of the day, but the joy of triumph in battle and giving my life as a martyr for the cause of our team was sweet consolation to my shaken soul. I had tagged a man in stink base that had once shot a bear, so I relished the victory for all it was worth—and then some.

Chapter Fourteen:

I Was Born With It

This memoir of my life from birth to age eighteen would not be honest or complete without connecting my youth to my chosen life profession. My LDS mission and my experience in the seminary and institute program profoundly influenced my decision to become a religious educator. My seminary and institute instructors were my role models in this pursuit: George Anderson in junior high school; Jim Carver and Ron Bradley in high school; and Garth Monson, Ken Jackson, Roy Hatch, and LeMar Hanson at the Ephraim LDS Institute of Religion.

After becoming a seminary teacher, my first assignment was in Lehi, Utah, where I taught at the senior seminary for fourteen years and then at the junior seminary for nine years. I served as seminary principal for the latter fourteen years. I then moved to Wisconsin. I served for fourteen years as director of the institute adjacent to the University of Wisconsin in Madison and as the coordinator of seminaries and institutes throughout Wisconsin and Upper Michigan. In this latter assignment, I drove an estimated 350,000 miles administering seminaries and institutes, training and supervising teachers, and teaching classes. A few years ago, I calculated the number of individual class sessions I have taught to be approximately 20,586. I am blessed to have had these countless opportunities to teach and testify of the restored gospel of Jesus Christ. I have often been asked how and when I gained my testimony. I reply, "I was born with it."

This testimony has matured and continues to guide my life and my teaching. I have lived and taught these past several years in a hotbed of atheism. Our city is headquarters to the Freedom From Religion Foundation, and it is home to a whole bunch of other non-believers of every variety. I have gained a healthy respect for science, believing much of what they say. I just feel they could do so much better if a testimony of the true nature and plan of God were their foundational truth rather than their nemesis (And I am grateful for the many good scientists who do have and exercise testimonies of religious truth).

In a seminary class I recently taught, we reviewed the arguments of the anti-Christ Korihor, who purported, "Ye cannot know of things which ye do not see."[24] We discussed how much the students had used electricity since they awoke in the very early morning and how much it had blessed their lives, and yet not one of them could claim they had seen it. I shared with them my experience a few years ago when I read several of the books and watched the debates of the atheists. I came away feeling sad for them—had they grown up with believing parents and great gospel friends, leaders, and teachers, perhaps they would have drawn correct conclusions.

Much of my childhood centered on the Fairview South Ward church building—the back lawn was our sandlot, the creek was my playground, and the Relief Society rooms were my second home as I accompanied my mother in her countless hours of service as the ward rug loom manager. I collected the empty spools from the loom as my toys. I crawled around under the quilt frames as the ladies quilted. And through it all, there was a great spirit of truth permeating the place.

Primary was held on a weekday right after school. In summer, I grumbled some at having to leave the adventures of the hayfield or the barnyard where I was working with Dad when my mother would honk the horn to take me to Primary, but once I got there, I felt the spirit of the place and loved learning the gospel from such dedicated teachers as Ila Jensen, Stella Seeley, and Helen Bohne. I have vivid memories of decorating my bike to ride in the Primary parade or constructing a diorama of a pioneer village while learning of the faith of our ancestors.

On clear days, we could hike to the top of the hill at our farm or climb upon our big rock and look away thirty miles to see the Manti Temple. One Easter, Mom took us to the temple grounds where we rolled our Easter eggs down the steep west lawn. There was something about the temple that seemed to beckon to me. Later when I was able to go inside, I was able to connect the feelings of my youth with my developing knowledge and understanding of doctrinal truth.

When I was eight, I was baptized at the Fairview South Ward by Leon Nielsen in the basement font—now filled in and serving as a coat closet. I have always wondered why Dad did not do it and perhaps will ask him someday on the other side. Perhaps it was just convenience—Leon was already wet from baptizing Karen, so he just baptized me also.

As a young deacon, I remember going to sacrament meeting early and just sitting in the chapel. I had inherited my mother's inclination for people watching, but I also enjoyed how I felt while I was there. I enjoyed my responsibilities of passing the sacrament. One Saturday, our quorum took a trip to Temple Square and someone with connections to people in high places arranged for us to visit the office of President David O. McKay. We had hoped he would be there to greet us and were disappointed that he was not. But I got to sit in his chair. As I did so, I just knew that he was who and what I had been taught he was. Those feelings for the Lord's living prophets have never left me.

I memorized the Articles of Faith, although I struggled with understanding the one about being "chased by an elephant" until I read it more slowly and carefully—"We believe in being honest, true, chaste, benevolent . . ."[25] I was proud to earn my Duty to God award and grateful for those who encouraged me to do so. During my first year of seminary, Prophet George, as we affectionately referred to our caring teacher, encouraged us to read the Book of Mormon. Although I did not really grasp it very well at the time, I felt the spirit of the book. Now that I have a somewhat better grasp of it, I continue to feel its spirit. As I have heard the arguments of its many critics—people often educated far beyond their intelligence—I marvel that their criticism is so trivial and does not even slightly mar or mutilate the central focus and doctrine of the book: Jesus Christ is the divine Son of God and He effected a perfect Atonement for us.

We were blessed to have inspired bishops to lead and guide us, such as Clyde Cox, Otis Nielsen, Reed Lasson, Henry Wheeler, and Leon Nielsen. They were humble and diligent, worked hard at their professions, and gave willingly of their time to help and inspire us to goodness. They were practical—I received a bishop's interview on one occasion in a dairy barn as the bishop milked his cows while counseling me on avoiding the perils of temptation. I have been guided through my life from the inspired and prophetic patriarchal blessing I received as a young teen at the hands of Brother Heber Mower.

I loved to hear the reports of returning missionaries. They instilled in me a desire to serve one day. The testimonies of Bill Cox, Bryan Shelley, and George Bench stand out vividly in my memory as worthy representatives of many who testified of their experiences and encouraged me to seek full-time missionary service. In recent visits to Fairview, I have delighted in reconnecting with so many who influenced my young life for good. I recall with gratitude how Mike Aime took me with him to Salt Lake City to attend an LDS servicemen's conference. He was a returned missionary and was headed for full-time military service in Korea. I had not yet served a mission and was headed for army basic training. I was so grateful for his encouragement of me and of his example of faith and goodness. I delight today to find him "still [my brother] in the Lord."[26]

There were a few "eyebrow raisers" in growing up among everyday, real-world saints, and as I was far from perfect myself, I think I better appreciated the circumstances. My brother Ron was not active in the church. We loved to fly fish at Fairview Lakes in the late evenings until it became too dark to see. Our sacrament meetings were held in the evenings back then. I was lured to our pleasures—I knew I was to honor the Sabbath, but I also loved to fish with my brother. So when Ron invited me to go fishing on Sundays, I wanted to skip my evening meeting, but my mother insisted that I attend. On a few Sundays one summer, we compromised. I attended the meeting and at the moment the final amen was uttered, I dashed out the door, ran the block to my home, changed my clothes, and jumped into Ron's truck. One of the great gospel mysteries of my young life occurred one Sunday evening as a counselor in the bishopric who also loved to fish at the lakes in the evenings conducted the meeting. I followed my usual routine of running home and riding with Ron to the lakes.. When we got there, the counselor in the bishopric was already there with his line in the water. How could this be? How could he have possibly beaten us there? Had he slipped out during the closing prayer? I did not notice. Someday perhaps I will ask him.

My introduction to home teaching was most definitely atypical. As a young man of fourteen, I was assigned to be a junior partner to Brother Alton Jones, with whom I served for a few years. Alt was a colorful character who had worked for the railroad most of his adult lifetime. At the time, he was the district foreman and my friend who worked for him one summer described him as no-nonsense—he said that when Alt came around, you were to keep your head down, keep your mouth shut, and keep on working. Perhaps that was more of an on-the-job persona, for I found Alt to be jovial and personable. But nothing seemed to embarrass or intimidate him. He served as the ward clerk for as long as I can remember. He also took care of the ward welfare project—a herd of cattle he kept on property just over the San Pitch west of our home. I delighted in working with him hauling hay, building or repairing fences, and branding the cattle.

In our years of home teaching, I do not think we ever missed a month. Alt would call and say, "Let's go get our home teaching done early so we can catch Bill out in the barn." I always wondered why this was important until one day when we visited him in his house. Bill lived alone—except for his chickens and who knows what else that lived in the house with him. We always encouraged our folks to attend church—none ever did. I sometimes joked that we were assigned to the less active members to keep them inactive. Our visits followed a routine. After reminding them to attend church, Alt reminisced with them about the good old days and told of his adventures growing up and working on the railroad, complete with the colorful vernacular of the settings. After we all had a good laugh or two, Alt would thank the folks for the visit and then he would offer a rote prayer petitioning the blessings of heaven to be upon them.

One evening, we visited a lady who had married and divorced a few times in a rather brief period after her first husband's death. I'll call her Sister Smith. Alt was zooming along just fine in his prayer until he came to her name, which he had forgotten. He said, "And bless Sister"— and then came a long, quiet pause. I was so embarrassed and wished I could whisper "Smith" to him. But Alt just looked up, opened his eyes, and asked, "Just what is your name this month?" She replied, "Smith." Alt concluded, "Oh yes, and bless Sister Smith! Amen." All was well. No one, except me, seemed troubled—especially not Alt.

Through the years since my youth, I have had, as we all do, opportunity to intermingle with many colorful characters living out diverse personalities and varied interpretations of life and doctrine. I often think of a quote attributed to President Brigham Young: "To live with saints in heaven is bliss and glory—to dwell with them on earth it quite a different story."[27] I have enjoyed my association with such honest, sincere, and hard-working people as Alt. Others have tried my faith and my patience. I am grateful that, through it all, I was born with a testimony of the gospel and I am confident that, in the Lord's eternal realm, each of us will be given ample opportunity to grow into our potential as children of a true and loving Heavenly Father.

Fairview with east mountains in background

Fairview museum (formerly Reg's kindergarten school)

Fairview South Ward church

Iven Cox memorial at city park

Steep farm lane

Grandpa and Grandma Christensen home in Fairview

Old Fairview roller mill

Reg's childhood home

Reg's first car

Boots Christensen splitting firewood

Boots and Elna Christensen at Wagon Wheel Campground in one of his restored buggies

Tucker Grandparents:
Mary Malinda and Francis Marion

Boots and Reg transporting calf to the farm in a boblsled

Reg's parents and siblings: L-R Ron, Charlie, Norma, Reg, Lowell

Reg sitting on Charlie's lamb

Reg in military

Reg on bicycle for Pioneer Day parade

Reg as Indian in Pioneer Day parade

Reg's 4-H garden

Historical marker for the Given Family Massacre

Fairview Harmonica Band: L-R Hugh Anderson, Alta Osborne, Mont Nordstrom, Boots Christensen, Sarah Gardner, Fred Gardner, Maitland Graham

Reg with church brethren at Boot's sheep camp on post-cutting activity

Borax 20 Mule Team at Wagon Wheel Campground

Sign-post from Wagon Wheel Campground

Chapter Fifteen:
The Cold War Comes to Fairview

A few years ago, I was informed and fascinated by reading a book about one of the "fathers" of the atomic bomb.[28] I learned that many of the scientists of the Manhattan Project had vivid inklings of the horrific potential of their work, but their consolation was that if anyone were to ever actually use what they were constructing, it would be so terrible that it would scare war out of men's hearts forever. Any sane person would have agreed with them, but sadly, they were wrong about this insane world of ours. We did use the bomb to deliver the knockout punch to World War II, and fortunately it has never been used since as a war weapon. But although the bombings of Hiroshima and Nagasaki were horrendous on a scale never before imagined, we went on making nuclear bombs. Our war went from hot to cold—from actually using the bomb to just threatening to do so.

This era of Cold War was such a crazy time in our world. Now that we had unleashed the bomb once, the possibility of doing so again became very real. There were many players in this battle of nerves, but I discerned from the newspapers I delivered each morning that the two major parties were the United States and the Soviet Union. I had fought in our neighborhood "chestnut" wars and knew that things could escalate rather quickly if our parents did not intervene. Where were the mothers of Nikita Khrushchev and Fidel Castro and why did they not send their bad boys to their rooms to cool off? But no, they kept spewing forth their scary rhetoric, unnerving adults and frightening little kids like me. Why did Nikita say he would bury us? What had we done wrong? Why did the Russians hate us when they had not even met us? Why didn't they just come over for a visit and let us show them around our town and introduce them to our folks? Then they would know that we did not want to fight them. But no—we fixated on war and mass destruction.

World leaders struggled and plotted to figure out how to deliver their bombs remotely without flying pilots over enemy lands. The Russians won the first official round of the growing "space race" on

October 4, 1957, by launching a low-earth orbit of a four-pronged bas-ketball-like device called Sputnik—the first ever artificial earth satellite. Four years later, John F. Kennedy, our daring young president, countered the Soviet's success in space with his own challenge: "I believe that this nation should commit itself to achieving the goal, before this decade is out, of landing a man on the moon and returning him safely to earth."[29] This bold move came on the heels of our failed attempt to overthrow the Cuban government just the month previous in the Bay of Pigs fiasco. The next year, Khrushchev and the Soviets took advantage of our failure and began installing missiles in Cuba, believing that Kennedy was weak and inexperienced and would not dare counter their efforts. But President Kennedy rose to the occasion by imposing a naval and air blockade around Cuba. When the Soviets shot down one of our spy planes, tensions escalated to fever pitch. The thirteen-day standoff known as the Cuban Missile Crisis brought the Cold War as close to the brink of turning hot as it ever was. Gratefully, President Kennedy kept his head clear and played a cool hand—even after our plane was shot down. The Soviets finally backed down and the world breathed a sigh of relief.

So how did we handle the Cold War in Fairview? We worried about it. We were swept up in the efforts of the nation to educate us and prepare us for the possibility of nuclear war. Children everywhere were being taught "duck-and-cover" tactics—wherever you were and whatever you were doing, you would "stop, drop and cover."[30] The humble turtle was the role model—in danger, he stops all activity and pulls into his protective shell.

We enhanced our food and water storage and made assessment of our homes and root cellars to determine how we might seal ourselves off from the world for an extended period in case of need. We prayed for peace. We sought out the counsel of our spiritual leaders. We discussed world events with fellow saints and neighbors in our meetings and over back fences.

Our local government organized and planned what we could do to better protect our community. Dad was appointed as the civil defense chairman for our neighborhood and even went to Camp Williams for a whole week for training in nuclear weaponry and how to protect citizens against its effects. Plans for neighborhood "fallout shelters" were shared. He came home nervous about the growing threat but prepared to begin plans and actions for protection. He talked to neighbors and prompted them to assess their circumstances. It was a real and a tense time in our lives. The Cold War scared us.

I had a growing, innate uneasiness in my small child's heart that these efforts were all in vain. I sensed that that if and when atomic bombs were dropped, the consequences would be more terrible than anyone realized and that our lives on this earth would be over. That thought saddened and frightened me. I was thus grateful for the wisdom and counsel of some who were older and wiser, such as Ross Cox and Lewis (Lew) Rigby.

Ross Cox and his wife Armada lived in Ephraim and were the proprietors and editors of the local newspaper there. He had experienced war, having fought in France in World War I. He later served as the mission president of the Hawaiian Islands during World War II and was there when Pearl Harbor was attacked. One day, he was guest speaker in our ward sacrament meeting and spoke in somewhat light and chiding terms of the space race, counseling us not to worry too much about the "Spudnut" that the Russians had launched (A "Spudnut" was a popular donut of the times made from potato flour). He assured us that the Lord was in charge and that His purposes would be fulfilled and that the wicked of the earth would be handled in His way and time.[31]

Lew Rigby was our neighbor—his home was in the center of the block, just across the street just to the north and east from our property. He was a brother to old Doc Rigby and his wife, Ione, was the sister of my Uncle Jack Sanders, who was married to Dad's sister, Venna. So I claimed Lew as nearly my own relative—and he always made me feel as though I was. In fact, those who remember Lew describe him as one of the nicest, friendliest, happiest, most genuine people they have ever known. He cared for people. He carried no pretense about him—he was plain-spoken and comical. One day he said to Dad, "By gads, Boots, there are sure a lot of people dying that never died before." On another occasion, when old Lester gave an extraordinarily long prayer to end sacrament meeting, Lew said to his niece at dinner, "Reva, I want Lester to give the closing prayer at my funeral and, by gads, after he has prayed for an hour, if he hasn't got me into heaven, let me go to hell." He said what he thought and likely offended some, but most of us found it refreshing.

Lew had a very distinctive and comical gait, with an exaggerated swinging of his arms on a bit of a sideways slant. We recognized him walking along well before we could see his face. I do not know when he gave up driving a car, but as long as I knew him, he motored around town in a funny-looking little three-wheeled golf cart. One of my favorite boyhood delights was when Lew would stop and give me a ride, which he often did. I think he even let me drive it around the church a few times.

Lew was born in 1892 and had thus lived through two world wars and countless other conflicts and world events. He had his trials, I am sure. I do not know much of his younger life but sensed that he had been schooled by hard knocks. He was somewhat annoyed by the two quint-essential town busybodies who lived on opposite ends of his block. Lucy and Delta were fine ladies who did much good for the community—they just liked to be informed about everyone's business and did not hold back from offering a running commentary.

Lew worked as the custodian of the junior high school and, later, as the custodian of our Fairview South Ward church building. He was practical and inventive. I well remember the fun I had when he would let me ride for a bit behind him on the little wheeled cart he had made to tow himself behind the big reel lawnmower as he mowed the large church lawns. From scratch, he constructed a large contraption that looked like a squirrel cage on the backside of the building that served well as a swamp cooler for the chapel on warm summer evenings. He seemed able to fix anything.

I loved Lew's gift for speaking plainly. One morning I happened into the post office, a sort of informal community gathering place, when Lew was there and Bishop Otis Nielsen came in. He thanked Lew for the purchase of some lightbulbs for the church and asked if he would like to be reimbursed or if he would rather just have the blessings. Lew replied, "By gads Bishop, I believe I will take the reimbursement. I have so damned many blessings piled up now that I don't know what to do with them all." That was Lew. He called things as he saw them—nothing more and nothing less.

Lew always sat on the end seat of the back row of the chapel during sacrament meeting. After the sacrament was passed, he would slip quietly out of the meeting to go stoke the old coal furnace in wintertime or to check the water flow on his swamp cooler in summertime. And everyone who really knew him also knew that, after he checked on things, he hiked up to the Travel Inn Café for his morning coffee before slipping quietly back into his pew just before the benediction.

One morning, during the height of the Cold War frenzy, I went into the post office with Dad and Lew was there picking up his mail.

Dad suggested to Lew the possibility of a neighborhood fallout shelter where folks would congregate for a few weeks with food and water until the nuclear danger passed. Lew, after a long and thoughtful pause, said, "By gads, Boots, if I have to choose between a nuclear bomb or being cooped up for two weeks with Lucy and Delta, I think I will just take my chance on the bomb. But, thanks anyway and best to you."

It would yet be nearly three more decades before President Ronald Reagan would visit the Berlin Wall and then stand at the Brandenburg Gate and deliver what was effectively the knockout punch of the Cold War with his strong challenge to the leader of the Soviet Union, "Mr. Gorbachev, tear down this wall!" But as far as my own perception of the threat of Fairview's nuclear annihilation went, Lew Rigby had pretty well put things in proper perspective for me. I realized that we would likely survive and that the world would keep on turning for a while yet. I felt a calm sense of peace as was I watched Lew comically shuffle over to his golf cart and, with a wry, triumphant smile on his face, drive away.

Chapter Sixteen:
An Authentic Indian

On Saturday July 24, 1847, the vanguard company of the Mormon pioneers exited Emigration Canyon and paused at the crest of small hill. President Brigham Young, who was ill from mountain fever, briefly rose from his wagon sickbed, surveyed the barren sagebrush flats of the Salt Lake Valley and proclaimed, "It is enough. This is the right place. Drive on."[32] With this declaration, President Young affirmed the prophetic vision he had seen of their new homeland shortly after their exit from Nauvoo.

In President Young's vision, he saw an angel standing on a cone-shaped hill pointing out to him where the temple was to be built. On Sunday, the small pioneer company worshipped and kept the Sabbath. On Monday, July 26, President Young and other leaders climbed this conical hill overlooking the valley and in a symbolic gesture of gathering Israel, waved a banner in fulfillment of Isaiah's prophecy: "And he will lift up an ensign to the nations from far, and will hiss unto them from the end of the earth: and, behold, they shall come with speed swiftly."[33] Shortly after he descended Ensign Peak, President Young thrust his cane into the desert soil and proclaimed "Here we shall build a temple to our God!"[34]

From the time of this first entrance of the pioneers into the Salt Lake Valley, July 24 has been known as Pioneer Day and has been celebrated with gratitude and enthusiasm throughout the Mormon settlements each year since. On July 24, 1857, Brigham Young and a few thousand saints were camped near Silver Lake in Big Cottonwood Canyon commemorating ten years of toil and sacrifice in their new land. In the midst of their celebrations with music of brass bands, speeches, and prayers of thanksgiving, Porter Rockwell and others rode into the camp to inform them that an army of the United States was headed for Utah to put down the so-called "Mormon Rebellion." After the festivities ended, the saints broke camp and went home to face this new challenge, which would plague them for several years until the army was recalled to the east at the outbreak of the Civil War.

Along with the annoyance of dealing with the US Army, the settlers faced the hardships of settling wilderness as they battled fire, crickets, apostasy, resettlement, drought, persecution, thirst, hunger, wind, snow, and disease. They struggled to live in peace with the Indians throughout the Utah Territory and sought to follow President Young's counsel of "feed them, don't fight them" and "biscuits, not bullets."

Four of the larger settlements of North Sanpete—Mt. Pleasant, Fairview, Moroni, and Spring City—seemed to have long-standing agreement that two would host Independence Day celebrations and two would host Pioneer Days, each supporting the others. Fountain Green continued their annual Lamb Days tradition. Fairview's time to shine was Pioneer Day, which was, and I think still is, a big deal. Personally, I always ranked it a close second to Christmas.

The parade and the rodeo were the highlights of the day for me. The rodeo grounds were on the cemetery road adjacent to the west side of the baseball field and grandstand. Cowboys from around the state would congregate to test their nerve against the bulls and broncos. One year, an angered bull jumped the fence and raised some havoc around the town before it was finally captured and returned to its keepers.

Of course, like many boys, I dreamed of someday being a rodeo cowboy. This dream had some fulfillment when the organizers began a kids' rodeo prior to the main event. I was thrilled beyond expression when I was seated on and tied to the back of a wild steer and heard my name announced over the loudspeaker. I rode high and proud with hardly a challenge from the ferocious critter—until someone opened the chute gate. At that point, I panicked and feared for my life as the side-winding steer bucked and jumped and tossed in every direction—but that was just in my imagination. I am sure the reality was that I rode the gently running beast for a while and then just kind of lost balance and fell off into the soft dirt. However, I was successful in convincing Dad to help me reenact the experience in our own corral with one of our own steers, but we soon tired of this adventure when I realized that the rocks, cedar trees, and barbed wire fences of our enclosure were not nearly as conducive to my enjoyment as the relatively safe and well-constructed rodeo arena. Plus, we had no cheering audience to encourage me.

Early each Pioneer Day morning, the city fathers drove around announcing the events of the day from extra noisy loudspeakers mounted on car tops and setting off charges of dynamite to ensure that the whole town would be awake and ready to celebrate. After a pancake breakfast in the park, we congregated in the church for an inspirational and patriotic speech delivered by an invited guest. After the parade, an array of kids' activities were held throughout the afternoon. We could test our skills at pioneer games, greased pole climbing, and greased pig chasing. If we reached the top of the pole, we kept the dollar bill fastened there. Whoever caught the pig kept it too—I sure tried, but never succeeded. I felt like I had won the lottery one year when I retrieved a ping pong ball dropped from an airplane, which allowed me to receive a free package of cream cheese from the Merc. After the rodeo, impressive fireworks adorned the night sky to conclude the day.

Friends and relatives carrying food and drink gathered on our front lawn on south Main Street to view the parade. Bands played. Dancers danced. Horses pranced as cowboys rode in proud array. Clowns made us laugh. Soldiers marched. The Riding Club drilled their horses in occasional figure eights. Everyone stood with hands over hearts in reverent silence as the flag passed. Grand marshals called out kind greetings to old friends. Politicians threw candy. Beauty queens waved and smiled. Pioneers and mountain men reenacted their crafts. The Harmonica Band played their tunes from a flatbed truck or a horse-drawn band wagon. Frank Larsen tap danced. Cheerleaders twirled and strutted. Kids rode their bikes and trikes decorated with crepe paper up and down and all around. Fire engines screeched. Manure spreaders did nothing, fortunately, except just keep moving along. Army trucks and guns passed in proud review.

Mom loathed the limelight and would never ride in a parade—her pleasure was in organizing the food and seating for our front-lawn guests. Dad was always on display in some fashion or another—generally with the Harmonica Band. I always delighted in helping him and his friends in their parade preparations. I recall at least a few occasions I was filled with pride when my advice to them proved helpful. One year, they constructed a sagebrush float—in fact, they did so several years. After they loaded rocks and logs on their flatbed wagon and arranged the freshly cut sagebrush, they decided they would light a real fire with real smoke. I happened to remember the bottom portion of an old steel barrel out behind our barn and dragged it to them, to their delight. It worked great for an in-transit fire pit. On another occasion, they built their float in Golden Carlson's driveway, constructing extended wings on the wagon to hold the sagebrush. When I posed the question of whether or not it would now fit through the driveway gate, they had to decide whether to remove the float wings or the steel center post of the gate. They opted for the post so they could accommodate future dilemmas.

I loved riding my horse and, thankfully, I always had a horse to ride in my childhood—Old Blaze, a sorrel mare, in the early years, and then Candy and Chief, a matched palomino team in later years. The palomino team also pulled our larger wagons and winter bobsled. After I left home, Dad opted for a smaller team of Welsh ponies to pull his lighter buggies and wagons—Dusty and Dan were our matched pair.

One year when I was about ten, I felt the yearnings of independence. I had tired of the boring riding of my bike in the Pioneer Day parade with its crepe paper–woven wheels and handlebar tassels. I plotted a solo ride on Old Blaze. I wanted to be an authentic Indian like the ones I had seen on TV. For weeks, I planned and plotted my performance. I could certainly not be authentic if I used a saddle and bridle and reasoned that I would be just fine without a bit in the mouth of Old Blaze. I made my own hay string hackamore with a single rein. After all, her home was our barn and the horse pasture adjacent to the north of our home.[35] Since Old Blaze lived in "the city," she was accustomed to the roaring of truck engines, the honking of car horns and the very rare fire or police siren. She would do fine in the parade!

On parade day, I donned my gunny sack britches, smeared my skin with cocoa powder, and fastened a lone feather into my leather headband. I then looped my crude hackamore around the nose of Old Blaze and off I went. In those days, the parade formed in the south near our home and traveled north until it disbanded at the beginning of the Milburn Road. I am not sure how, but I won a coveted parade spot not far behind the grand marshal. Perhaps they had not yet discovered the science of placing of horses at the end of the parade. Or, perhaps my authenticity and creativity had earned me the prime spot. All was grand. I stealthily rode along, scouting for varmints and occasionally waving at friends and acknowledging comments from my many admirers. It was one of the greatest days of my young life.

As I approached the Skyline Motel near the end of the parade route, I spotted some of my Salt Lake cousins. The excitement of the day was about to reach its zenith. One of the cousins decided it would be clever to throw a bundle of firecrackers into the street as I passed by. As the explosions began, Old Blaze, with one mighty yank of her head, threw off the loosely wrapped hackamore and almost threw me off in the process. In panic, I clutched hard at her mane and held on for dear life as she whirled and, in a blaze of glory, began her frightened gallop for the home pasture. Cars swerved. Clowns ran. Armies retreated. Cheerleaders squealed. The most memorable moment was when we headed straight at the marching band. In a startled panic, they, clutching their instruments, split like the Red Sea when Charlton Heston as a majestic Moses parted its great waters on the big screen. It was magnificent!

Luckily, I hung on for the duration. Once we were home and Old Blaze was calmed, safe and free in the pasture, I began thinking about the next year. I thought I might get some crepe paper and decorate my bike once again.

Chapter Seventeen:

Laugh Festivals—Tucker Style

Whenever I got word that my out-of-town Tucker aunts and uncles had arrived at Grandpa and Grandma's place, soon to be joined by the locals, I got on my bike or saddled my horse and rode there as fast as I could. I got my hug from Grandma, helped myself to a donut or brownie that Aunt Unalee brought from the bakery where she worked, found my perch halfway up the spindled stairwell where I could see both the kitchen and the living room, and watched the show that would go on through the evening. And what a show it was! I think these were the funniest people I have ever met (and I must concede two things in retrospect—I was biased, and some of the entertainers were influenced by performance-enhancing alcohol). At mealtime, everyone gathered to the huge round kitchen table for a potluck. We kids would go around the table to get our food and then the first two would climb to the top of the stairs and sit on the top step, continuing with two on every other step all the way down.

During a Christmas gift exchange, someone found a lone gift way back under the tree tagged for Donna. When she opened it and discovered a live mouse in a mason jar, she let out a squeal that could be heard across town. Another time, while playing hide-and-seek with the cousins, we were told a bat was hiding under the upstairs bed, only to discover a baseball bat—Grandma's prank on us.

My Tucker grandparents were blessed to have nine of their eleven children live to adulthood. Aunt Donna's grandkids once wrote a song about them, using nicknames for some, which has been sung over the years (their real names in birth order are Clea, Winn, Ruby, Elna, Floyd, Jack, Donna, Ralph, and Unalee). The song went like this:

It started out a long, long time ago—In this little town of ours

Chorus:
Tummy, Pinto, Ruby, Fanny, Floyd, Poncho—
Donna, Doc, and Unalee, and more.
Tummy, Pinto, Ruby, Fanny, Floyd, Poncho—
Donna, Doc, and Unalee, and more (End Chorus)

They had some problems, short of money, but they were full of
love, and that's what it takes to build a family.
A family they did have!

(Repeat Chorus)
We take our hats off to them; salute their bravery and their love to
everybody here. And look what we got now. They got me and they
got you and they got more.

What?! They got more?

(Repeat Chorus)

Of course, as is generally true with storytelling, the stories seemed
to improve with age—but not much with this group—they were pretty
good already. Unalee and Donna seemed to be the two shining stars in
funniness, often narrating each other's antics. On one trip to Fairview,
Unalee was catching a ride with someone and Leon, her husband, would
come later after work. She needed to hide some cash for him at home,
which she did in a dresser drawer. When Leon got home, he found
a note taped to the front door, "Leon, I hid the money in the dresser
drawer."

My mother once drove her sisters from Fairview to Sunnyside to
visit Clea and Manuel and Floyd and Sally. They talked and laughed so
hard that they missed the Sunnyside turn and went all the way to Green
River before they even considered that they might be lost. For the rest of
my mother's life, anytime her siblings knew she was driving someplace,
they would always inquire if she were going via Green River. They also
laughed at her when they reminisced about when she was a little girl and
Winn persuaded her to crawl into an old car tire that he subsequently
rolled off the roof of the chicken coop.

Unalee did not drive until after Leon died. She then timidly learned what she needed to know and would add extra miles to her trek due to her phobia of left turns. She soon lived in a world of right turns only and was doing fine until it was time to put gas in the car. She did fine with figuring out that there was a gas cap on the car, and she even removed the pump nozzle and inserted it into the car, but she could not get the pump to work. When the helpful attendant spoke to her through the intercom, "Lift the arm" (referring to the handle or "arm" on the pump), she lifted *her* arm with the nozzle in her hand. The attendant must have sensed her fun spirit and played the scenario for all it was worth. "No, higher," he said and Unalee lifted the nozzle even higher into the air. But she still could not get it to pump gas. After Unalee's command performance in reenacting the story for a few years, her sisters even procured an old gas pump nozzle and gave it to her for her birthday as a memorial of her experience.

When Donna and Art lived in Las Vegas, they took Grandpa Tucker to a downtown show of scantily glad girls. When he fixated in amazement on the scenes, they teased him that they were going to tell his bishop. But he was not fazed. "Oh," he said, "even a bishop would like that show." They kidded him about that for the rest of his life. One of the more memorable highlights of our get-togethers was when Grandpa would bring out his guitar and sing the old minstrel songs.

Once while hunting deer, Grandpa and the boys were in a long line, with Winn at the top, making a drive up through the trees. Suddenly the man at the bottom of the line called out, "Here comes a big elk." This information was repeated man to man up the chain until it got to Winn. After a pause—BANG! This became one of those stories that grew with the years, I am sure, but we all laughed at the predicament that Winn had put himself in by shooting an elk during deer season. But the silver lining to the cloud was that in their day of scarcity, they made the best of their misfortune and stored the bonus meat away for winter.

Unalee once had a small stove fire and hurriedly called the fire department, giving them strict instructions to "Come easy [no lights and sirens] because it is just a small fire." On another occasion when she and Leon lived in a basement duplex apartment, she was outside one day and could not resist peeking in the neighbor's window, after which she declared, "Well, they don't have it any better than we do." She was disappointed to later discover that she had looked into her own window. Once, when someone suggested a trip to visit Mesa Verde National Park in Colorado, Unalee perplexedly quipped, "I do not think I know Mesa or Verde."

Uncle Jack Tucker was double-jointed. He could flex his ankles to turn his feet around and stand almost as though his feet were on backwards. To the delight of the kids, he would do so and then tell the story of when he was in the army and stood that way once for morning formation. Their commander was so impressed that he had the entire company file past and take a look.

Uncle Ralph amused everyone with his rendition of a popular song of the day, "I'm My Own Grandpa," about a man who, through an unlikely series of marriages, becomes stepfather to his own stepmother. As the song proceeds, the "step" is dropped and he eventually becomes his own grandfather.

A favorite pastime of the laugh festivals was reminiscing about the many years of Tucker reunions in Fairview's mountains. I have vague memories of a few of these gatherings in my early childhood. Mattresses were hauled to the site to make beds for everyone. One year, they made big iron letters to spell "Tucker," wrapped them in rags saturated with oil, strung them on a wire, and lit them on fire to be seen from miles around. They played softball and performed skits. My Tucker uncles, likely prompted by entertainment from their war-time service, dressed as hula girls with coconut brassieres and grass skirts and did a great job of bringing disrepute to the family name. Occasionally at our later reunions and laugh fests, the uncles reenacted their past performances. The dance or skit was not particularly amusing in itself, but the notion of a bunch of clumsy, old, bald, fat guys performing it made it memorable. Uncle Winn once wore Aunt Donna's wig and drunkenly danced a jig around the kitchen table.

One of my favorite stories is of when Dad was traveling to southern Utah for his insurance business and consented to drive Unalee on her first-ever trip across the Nevada desert to visit Donna in Las Vegas. She was amazed at the barren wasteland and commented, "Hey Boots, I wonder what kind of trees those are," referring to the cactus-like Joshua trees. Dad just casually commented, "Oh, those are macaroni trees." After a few contemplative moments, Unalee said, "Ya know, Boots, I don't think I realized until now that macaroni grew on trees." Dad replied, "Well, we learn something every day." I am not sure how long Unalee believed Dad's prank, but I am fairly certain that he exploited it for all it was worth. If she went to her grave with this misunderstanding, I would like to have been there when she learned the truth. And I suppose in the eternal realm, this will be a story retold forever at the Tucker Laugh Festival reunions. I am looking forward to them!

Chapter Eighteen:
The Stew Monument

Along with trying to be an authentic Indian, I often fancied myself as a great cowboy, riding off into the sunset with Roy Rogers, the Rifleman, or the Lone Ranger. I was disillusioned that I could never get Old Blaze or Candy or Chief to run for endless miles without tiring as with the TV horses, but I tried anyway on occasion. I soon settled into more passive and mellow pursuits, such as helping Frank Larsen herd his cows home from the pasture for the evening milking.

Frank was a fascinating old guy. Someone told me that he had been a muleskinner (one who drives mules) in WWI. I never talked with him much about that, but I did hear a story perhaps connecting his life back to his previous service as a mule handler. My brother Ron bought a house next to Frank and lived there for a few years until they bought their home in Spring City. My brother Charlie was visiting Ron one day and was in the side yard when Frank came along with his hay wagon drawn by two skinny and weak old plug horses. As they turned the corner and went down the lane adjoining Ron's yard, Charlie heard Frank holler, "Whoa, there, you fiery critters. Hold back now!" Charlie laughed because Frank's tired old horses were anything but fiery and were barely moving forward, leaning on each other for support—had they held back any more, they would have stopped. Frank was obviously daydreaming of his younger days of charging a team of strong mules through the battleground.

Frank kept his tired, skinny cows—seemingly the very ones from Joseph's dream in Egypt—in a pasture at the bottom of the lane that went from the home of Clyde Cox past Eugene Bohne's home and Melgaard's pond and ended down in the midst of farmer's fields a mile or so south of town. At the appointed hour, I would ride Old Blaze down the lane and pull up beside Frank. We would then ride along together herding the cows—which did not require much as the lane was well fenced on both sides. As Frank recounted the news of the day to me, I felt important and useful.

As we came to the area of the aforementioned pond, the cows would stop to drink from Spring Creek, which traversed the gravel lane through a buried steel culvert with an open area between the culvert ends and the fences. One day, a strange thing happened. As the cows stopped to drink, Frank dismounted from his sway-backed old horse and knelt to drink right with the cows. After a long drink, he raised up, wiped his chin on his sleeve, looked at me and said, "Young man, I would not trade a drink of this here water for a frosty mug of root beer from Floyd Young's drug store" (To me, it looked about the same).

When I got home, I told Dad of Frank's drink and he asked me a profound question: "Was he upstream or downstream from the cows?" And sure enough, as I considered the question, I realized that Frank had indeed been upstream just before the point where the water became troubled and mucky from the cows. I have told this story many times in my teaching and encouraged my students to always "drink upstream from the cows," suggesting ways they may do so. I have observed that there are a lot of people drinking downstream from the cows—politically, spiritually, intellectually, and socially. In retrospect, I realize what a great life lesson it was for me to serve as an apprentice cowboy to old Frank, if for nothing more than this life lesson.

Assisting Frank in herding his cows prepared me for greater cowboy adventures. When Big George Collard came to town, life became more interesting. He was a physical giant—I imagined that he must be Goliath's twin. He lived across the highway east of the Turpins where he built a home that he hoped to fill with a wife and children. He eventually did so. He built a huge fish pond. He seemed to have money and rumor was that he owned the mountains east of Fairview. He built a cabin near the Fairview Lakes. I think I first got acquainted with him as I worked with the Turpins on their dairy. He was eventually called as our young men advisor in church.

My first impression of Big George was that he was rather boorish and I felt some initial personality collisions with him. But, once I got to know him, I recognized his goodness and sincere motive. He was knowledgeable and talented and not afraid to try things. I learned a lot from him and soon felt a rapport with him. One of the best things I felt he did for our group of boys was our great cowboy adventure.

My horse adventures so far had been day activities—I had never actually gone on an overnight roundup or camping trip involving horses, even though I had thought about it and even planned such activities from time to time. The most adventurous trek I had taken to date was a day when I missed school and went with Dad and others from the ward seventies quorum on a Christmas tree cutting/ fundraising adventure, hauling the cut trees on our horses. I had found my way home on a lonely course away from the others and had to trust the horse to find the way as darkness came. So now that I was a seasoned veteran, as I assumed, I was delighted when Big George proposed taking a dozen or so of us on a week-long high adventure packing trip with our horses.

After procuring horses for the boys who had none and finding one big enough to carry George, we made our preparations and, on the appointed day, started up the face of the mountains with Fairview Lakes as our destination. This was a whole new world to be out and about for an extended time with so many boys and so many horses. Some of the boys were more seasoned in such matters and some had never really ridden horses much before in their lives. I, of course, had helped Frank herd his skinny cows up the fenced lane and had also survived the Pioneer Day parade, so I felt that I could handle anything that came our way on this open-range ride. We generally did well and got to our campsite the first day.

For several days, we hiked, fished, and swam in the lake. We cooked our meals over open fires and tended to our horses with advice and help from Big George (I had never worried much about my horse before once I turned it loose in the pasture and barnyard for the night). We now had to stake out the horses so they would not wander off and had to protect them from bears, lions, wolves, horse thieves, and general bandits.

One day we found an abandoned row boat in the lake sunk under several feet of water. We tied some long ropes to it and used our horses to pull it from the deep. It seemed like it would float, so we concocted some makeshift oars, assigned a couple of bailers with camp buckets, and headed across the lake. I am not sure who had to work the fastest— the oarsmen or the bailers. We played with the boat for a few days before we had to abandon it when we broke camp.

One of the memorable highlights of the trip—not the greatest, but memorable—was the special stew Big George made for us in a large kettle. He worked very hard on this delicacy and I do not recall the ingredients. I just know that it was awful. What it lacked for flavor, it compensated for in greasiness. I think we tried to eat it but without much success. I regret offending our leader by this action—we could have likely ingested it and lived. But we complained and that started a bit of a power struggle. The end result was that Big George threatened that if we did not eat it for supper, we would be eating it the next day.

In the night, a few of us sneaked around and stole the cooled stew pot and carried it down to the creek to pour it out. But it would not pour, so we pried it out with sticks and left it standing in the middle of the creek. We assumed that it would erode during the night and evidence of our crime would be swept away. The next morning, the stew was still freestanding smack in the center of the stream like some eerie monument. Our deed was discovered.

I have wondered over the years if our stew monument is perhaps still there. Whether it is or isn't, the thought of it brings remembrance of some great friends, fun horses, and a good-hearted leader who, like so many others, tried in his own imperfect but sincere way to teach, guide, and influence a bunch of rowdy boys. For all of them, I am grateful.

Chapter Nineteen:
Wagon Wheel Campground

One Saturday when I was a young father, Mom and Dad were visiting our family in Lehi and I took Dad with me to install carpeting for a customer of my part-time carpet sales and installation business. As Dad watched me work, he lamented, "Oh, do I ever wish I would have had a skill like this to support my family" (I often wished I had something less brutal to support mine, but was grateful for the skill and the business that supplemented my teaching profession for thirty-five years). Dad's statement has caused me much reflection over the years. I have thought of him and Mom and how they labored so hard at so many things to provide a good living for us. In my mind, they did an excellent job—they were enterprising and hard working. I have tried to express my gratitude to them for their success.

As a young married man, Dad ran an auto service station for several years. He operated a grain cleaning business just prior to and during the years of World War II. And then at some point, he was introduced to the insurance business and experienced success for many years traveling the areas of central and southern Utah. Along with his insurance work, we managed our small farm. Through all the years, he also dabbled in concrete construction and rough carpentry (and finish carpentry that often looked rough). Then, of a sudden, things changed with the insurance company. I am not sure just what happened, but it related to buyouts and mergers and soon Dad did not feel that he could transition his perceptions and values to the changing world of his profession, so he cashed out and quit.

I have some vague memories of this difficult transition when I was in junior high school, but my sister tells me of the dark depression and struggle Dad went through that winter—sitting for hours in his basement office wondering what to do and how to survive. My memories of this time were more of an exciting journey through the brainstorming of Dad's mind as I accompanied him in exploration of such things as a fast food franchise, an overnight trailer park/tourist attraction and even a visit to a beaver production farm. I voted for the beaver farm, being fascinated by the long concrete tanks full of eager beavers which I considered as rather exotic.

I do recall a day in late winter or early spring when Dad had struggled long enough. He got up one day and announced, "We are going to build!" I asked, "Build what?" and he replied that he was not sure, but that we were going to build something. And build we did. I do not recall when our old barn just north of the garage was dismantled, but I think it was gone by then. In the center of our horse pasture, we began digging footings. Since this construction site was on Main Street and in full view of our school bus stop, my friends on the bus were very inquisitive, asking what we were building. I told them I was not sure—we would just all need to be surprised together. In Dad's mind was forming a rather vague concept of an overnight trailer park for tourists. We would figure out the details as we proceeded, but the Wagon Wheel Campground soon began to take shape.

We were amazed at the interest this project sparked in the community. Our response to people's inquiries was that this would be an overnight trailer park where tourists could shower, rest, and wash their clothes with a couple of coin-operated washers and dryers. When that word got out, we were astonished by the number of folks who began asking if they would be able to use the washers and dryers—so our business plan began to evolve. After we had poured footings and before we had gone much further than that, we were digging once again for more footings to expand our original floor plan to accommodate a larger laundry area. We also made provision for a dry cleaning machine. The soon-to-be laundry and dry cleaner was to be the mainstay of our business and would prove to be a godsend to my parents for many years.

The construction process was high adventure for me. We did the work mostly ourselves, but got some ongoing advice from my cousin in Provo who was a general contractor. We arranged for his plumber to rough in all of our water systems. As the earth was still partly frozen when we got ready for rough plumbing and pouring the concrete floor, we thawed the ground by burning a bunch of car tires, to the consternation of the neighbors (and actually most of the town—and unbelievable by today's standard). Once the fire cooled, Dad had me ride our big palomino horse Candy around and around to compact the dirt.

Since we were now going to manage a laundry, we needed a large drain field for the waste water. We hired a backhoe to dig some long parallel trenches that we lined with rocks. I liked this phase because even though I could not legally drive a car, I was permitted to drive our little 8N Ford tractor. I made many trips to our property by the San Pitch to load and haul the rocks piled along the fence line. We had been growing and harvesting them for years not knowing that we would have important use for them someday. After lining the trench bottom with rocks, we installed drainage pipe, added straw and tar paper and more rocks, then back-filled the dirt. To extend our drain field, we even purchased a small piece of property directly across Main Street from our home and hired a company to miraculously punch a hole under the road without digging a trench. Dad and I then used a long steel bar to pry and slide a pipe through the hole and then connected it to more drain pipe on the other side.

We hired a local electrical contractor to help us install power hookups for the trailers and campers. We hired Woody Cox and his big truck to haul our lumber and trusses from Provo. Dad and I (my older brothers were gone from home by now) framed the building and installed the trusses. Dad did not really trust me much with his circular saw, but after we had installed the rustic exterior siding panels, I self-trained on the saw one day while the folks were away by making a fishing tackle box out of the siding scraps. I gratefully kept all of my fingers and the tackle box, which I still have today. From then on, I was permitted to use the saw with occasional supervision.

I felt important when Dad allowed me to hand-nail much of the roof with genuine hand-split, rustic cedar shake shingles that I just knew would last forever (though the current owners have now installed a metal roof). We finished the interior with a large main area for the laundry and a couple of restrooms. Dad worried for days about the prospect of cracking a long wall mirror when he would install it in the bathroom. Sure enough—WHAM! He made a huge crack with his hammer. But it was usable and added to the personality of the place (This may have been when I began to coin the phrase that I still use today when I do handyman stuff—"Hey, if you wanted it done right, you should have hired a professional").

On the center-front of the property, we erected our business sign by concreting a huge wagon wheel into the ground as a base (I can't imagine it has gone anywhere, as we anchored it pretty good). Our sign read, "Wagon Wheel Campground and Laundromat." We were soon to learn about trademarks and such and had to change "Laundromat" to "Coin-Operated Laundry" when we received a letter of complaint. We planted some small pine trees along the front—most, I believe, are still there.

We received and installed our laundry equipment and went to Salt Lake to attend a manufacturers' training on the care and repair of the washers, dryers, and dry cleaner. One thing apparently not covered in the session was the management of high pressure washer hoses. One slipped from my hands and sprayed one of our very first customers square in the face just as she entered the front door. But she dried off and forgave me and we were in business (From this experience I learned that it worked best to shut off the water supply *before* disconnecting the hose).

As we opened for business, we had a fun little rendezvous with pop culture. Dad advertised an open house and some folks stopped in to see our new business. Mike Blackburn, a popular and likable guy in our neighborhood and soon-to-be high school student body president, stopped by and sang a little song about Dad (Boots) that he had composed as a spoof on the popular song of the day "These Boots Are Made for Walkin'" by Nancy Sinatra. Mike's words went something like this: "These Boots are made for washin', and that's just what they'll do! One of these days these Boots are going to wash all over you. Get ready Boots—start washin'." There was another popular song entitled "Leader of the Pack" by a trio of gals called the Shangri-Las. A group named, of all things, The Detergents, had done a parody they called "Leader of the Laundromat." A few of my friends gave me the nickname "Leader," as in "Leader of the Laundromat." Fortunately the nickname did not stick.

We did some advertising and soon had some overnight trailers and campers pulling in to spend the night. One day Dad was out watering the front lawn with a hose when some folks towing a trailer house stopped and announced, "It is just like they said. We stayed in southern Utah last night and someone told us to drive north on Highway 89 until you come to an old farmer in bib overalls and a straw hat. Stay there for a great time!"

We tried to give them all a great time by visiting with them, taking them on a tour of our farm and community, and escorting them to the Fairview Museum. We constructed a bonfire pit encircled with benches, and adjacent to that, we built a rough shelter from cedar posts and a rustic roof to cover an old cook stove (We later moved this shelter and stove to our farm property where it was used for many more years for family and group socials). We used this stove and campfire area for church and community socials, and often our tourist guests would join in. We parked our old chuck wagon and sheep camp nearby so tourists could examine them and use them for photo ops. Sometimes we hooked up the horses to the buggy or wagon and gave rides. Through our business, we met interesting people from all over the country and tried to make them feel like friends. After they had stayed with us for a day or two, they were.

After some years, the overnight tourist venue evolved into more of a permanent, year-round trailer park for temporary construction or mine workers who wanted a place to stay for several months. The coin-op laundry developed into our main business. My mother managed much of this operation and would have me help her clean washers, make change for the patrons, and generally help run things. Each Saturday night, Mom and I would empty all of the laundry coin on our kitchen table, count and stack it and then roll it in coin papers to prepare it for deposit. This activity accentuated my coin collecting hobby.

In my junior high shop class, I had units on woodworking and leather craft. For my wood project, I constructed a glass showcase with a wooden frame and back locking doors. I really got into my leather craft unit and still occasionally hand-tool some special projects.[36] I really became passionate about this hobby one winter and used some of my paper route money to purchase my own tools and supplies. I set up a shop in our basement and spent every hour I could constructing leather projects from kits such as ashtrays, purses, wallets, belts, three-legged stools, and moccasins. During this time, I also made some freelance projects. We killed a beef cow that we had raised on our farm and Dad and I took the hide to a tannery. They tanned half of the leather for tooling and the other half for a pair of rough leather chaps Dad wanted me to make for him. From the tooling leather, I made two rifle cases lined with lamb's wool. I also hand-tooled the top-front and belt of the chaps with "Wagon Wheel Campground" and laced it to the rough leather. Dad was proud as could be.[37]

When summer came, Dad came to my school in Moroni to haul my showcase home from the shop. I proudly placed it in a corner of our building and stocked it full of all of my completed projects. I moved my leather shop from our basement to the old sheep camp so tourists could watch me work. Some did. I was encouraged as I began to sell a few of the items. And then on one fateful day, my enterprise pretty much ended. A rich tourist in a fancy Airstream trailer was staying with us and wanted to see my goods. With eagerness, I showed him what I had made and explained that, no, I did not have a warehouse inventory—what he was seeing was all that I had. Almost apologetically, he pulled out his wallet and bought my entire store. Obviously, I had underpriced everything. As he exited the building, he met Dad coming up the sidewalk and told him, "Well, I just put your son out of business." As I had many other adventures awaiting me, I was never able to fully replenish my showcase. I later donated it to the Fairview Museum.

One day, the front man for the famous 20 Mule Team of the US Borax Corporation contacted us to arrange an overnight stay at the Wagon Wheel for the mule team and all the handlers. They were on a cross-country promotional tour for their soap products. They also sponsored a popular TV program, *Death Valley Days*, hosted for a while by Ronald Reagan. I remember our excitement in the days awaiting their arrival. When the day came, they rode into camp and staked out all of the mules on the full length of the front lawn and then proceeded to pitch their tents, cook their meals, care for the mules, and respond to my endless questions about their fame and fortune (I do not recall if Ronald Reagan was with them, but I doubt it because if he was, no one mentioned it). Dad seemed to be in the height of his glory arrayed in his old bib overalls and straw hat and bantering with the cooks and muleskinners.

This occasion was a time of great pride and excitement for me. Just to think that the actual mules and people who were part of a weekly national television program were staying at our campground was perhaps, in my mind, the greatest event since the Harmonica Band had appeared on Eugene Jelesnik's *Talent Showcase*. But comical Uncle Winn Tucker seemed to keep things in perspective. It was all in fun, and we still laugh at his reflective insight. Aunt Carrie reported that as they had driven by and seen all of the white mules standing serenely across the lawn in the sunset, Winn casually commented, "Well, it looks like the Christensens are having a reunion."

Chapter Twenty:
An Overworked Guardian Angel

Years ago in my carpet business, I went to Salt Lake to pick up two gigantic rolls of heavy carpet for a house I had the contract for. I loaded them as I had done for several years—with one end of the carpet sitting on the huge wooden tool chest at the front of the truck bed and the other end resting atop the closed tailgate. The next morning, as I drove on a quiet street to work, the tailgate suddenly slammed open and the two huge rolls slid down and out onto the roadway. I shudder to consider what would have happened had the rolls fallen off on the freeway at rush hour the night before. I considered hiring an artist to paint my truck with a guardian angel flying behind with outstretched arms holding the rolls in place.

I do not espouse the notion that we each have a specific angel assigned just to us—but if we did, I think mine may have been overworked, especially during my childhood and teen years. I feel blessed that through it all, I have never had a broken bone nor required stitches for a wound (although my children tease me about all of the times I came home from carpet jobs revealing fingers wrapped with gauze of toilet paper and bandages of duct tape).

There were the natural, inherent dangers of a Fairview childhood, like rattlesnakes, ticks, and drinking bleach (they said that was why Cousin Reid's hair turned so white when they lived in our basement apartment). We got some ticks in our skin, but no lasting disease. I only recall two rattlesnakes at the farm and Dad took care of them before they devoured me.

I have mentioned riding on the hood of the 8N tractor, usually backwards. I spent many hours over many years in this activity and never once fell beneath the large (to a small boy) rear tires always staring me in the face. We often bounced over rocks or scraped under overhead tree limbs. I think I even fell a few times but was gratefully able to dodge the wheels. In hindsight, we could have so easily bolted or welded on a grab bar of some sort for me, but we never thought of it.

That same tractor was powerful enough to pull our hay wagons but did not quite have enough compression braking (which I think is a misnomer) to hold back the hay wagon as we drove down the steep hill at the farm ("Clements Lane," I think they called it—although it was made from an easement through our property). So we had some special steel wagon "shoes" made. When we got to the crest of the hill to begin our descent, we pulled the wagon into the shoes and chained the wheels fast so they could not turn. We then basically slid the wagon down the hill on the shoes. I think my cumulative experiences of rocking and rolling down that hill from my perch on top of the loads of hay explain why I have never felt much compulsion to spend a lot of time at amusement parks. They would pale in comparison to Dad dragging those hay loads down the hill.[38]

I recall when we were standing directly below the bulldozer that was constructing that lane as it was going along with one track up on the east bank. It teetered up onto the other track and almost tipped over towards us—but then settled back to normal position. My memory is of the rattled operator who could hardly stop shaking long enough to light his cigarette once he safely stopped and dismounted. We found our individual thrills many times by racing our bikes or sleds down this same hill.

For hay hauling on the San Pitch property, Dad constructed a "slip," which was basically a board platform laid flat on the ground. Since we did not need to transport the hay on the roads and did not need to go very far, the slip eliminated the need to lift the bales onto an elevated wagon. At the time of this experiment, I was too small to lift bales or drive the tractor, so my job was to climb all over everything and keep a general watch on the process. In doing so, I perched my feet on the front of the slip and leaned forward to hold onto the two arms of the chain pulling it. Dad was loading bales and Ron was driving the tractor. Then my feet slipped underneath the board slip. Dad now had the choice between saving my legs or stopping the tractor and getting it stuck in the mud. As we were driving through a wet area, I think Ron kept driving for a bit, but Dad soon stopped him. The soft mud had allowed my legs to sink down and slide along without injury, except my pride was a little hurt as Dad and Ron unloaded the bales to rescue me.

On another occasion, we had loaded a wagon of bales from a field out near the old stone quarry. I am not sure why we did this (we did not own property there), but David Evans was with us, so I think we may have been helping him and his dad. Dad was driving the tractor. David,

Ron, and I were on top of the load of bales as we went up an incline. I remember that they were teasing me by not letting me move to the front of the load, even though I was pleading with them in panic that the load was going to fall. I was right. I soon tumbled to the ground with bales falling all around and over me. Dad stopped the wagon. When he found me, I was just a foot or so from being run over by the wagon wheel. One advantage of this experience is that it served as a great learning hook years later when I heard the story of how Harry Truman did not want the job of vice president but was persuaded to take it. Just a few months later, he became the president of the United States upon the sudden death of President Roosevelt. The next day, President Truman told the Capitol Hill reporters, "Boys, if you ever pray, pray for me now. I don't know if you fellows ever had a load of hay fall on you, but when they told me yesterday what had happened, I felt like the moon, the stars, and all the planets had fallen on me."[39] I understood (in my own small way).

We had hours of fun in our barns—my earliest memories are from playing in the one adjacent to our home and garage. In our war games, we jumped from ledge to loft and traversed secret tunnels we made by moving hay bales around. We had a wool sacker—a large, elevated board platform with a significant opening in the center. Through this opening, we would suspend a long burlap wool sack that was held in place by a steel ring just larger than the hole. As we sheared the sheep, we would tie the fleeces and toss them up onto the platform. Then someone inside the sack would work his way up by tromping the fleeces tight until they reached the top. I recall one day when Dad was in the sack and I was throwing fleeces to him. He became claustrophobic and could not get out. I was too small to help him, and either he was too much of a tightwad to cut open the sack or he did not have a knife. In any event, I ran like lightning for help from a neighbor. I remember once when an older friend, Blake, was part of our games. He jumped for the hole of the wool sacker and hit the edge of it, cutting his bottom lip between his mouth and his chin clean through so he could stick his tongue out of the cut. That was one of the coolest things I had ever seen. I think he needed a few stitches to put it right.

Occasionally, dangers arose from the influence of TV. I assumed that my horse would do what the Hollywood stunt horses did. One day on my ride, I noticed a large, freshly cut tree limb lying by the side of the road a few blocks from my house and thought I had found a treasure. I went home, retrieved a long rope, went back, and secured the limb to my saddle horn. As soon as Old Blaze started out and sensed that something was chasing her, off she went. I think I was able to hold on to the saddle horn, but I got an exciting ride and provided a nice show for any observers along the way.

When I learned that I could throw a rock at the side of a certain chicken coop and elicit a unified mass clucking from the chickens, I made it a ritual whenever I would pass by. The first time I rode by on Old Blaze and threw my obligatory rock, I got more than I had bargained for. Although I maintained perfect form, position, and direction, Old Blaze jumped a good distance to the side and left me horseless in midair. As we have already established that Old Blaze had an excellent homing instinct, it should go without saying that the next time we met was at the home pasture.

I have already mentioned that my Stevens neighbors sold night crawlers, but we had another competitor—Byron Larsen, who lived on the corner to the south of us. He was not interested in hunting his worms at night, so he invented a daytime method that I copied. The method is very simple, although I would not recommend that anyone try this. Get two long steel rods with sharpened points and drill a small hole in the ends opposite of the points. Then take an electrical cord and split the two wires several feet apart. Attach the wires to the two holes in the steel rods and then drive the rods a few feet into the ground. Plug in the cord. Turn on the garden hose and let the water soak all around the poles, being careful to not place your hand in the steady water stream. You will soon have more worms than you could likely hope for. The only problem I recall from this method was one day when I forgot to unplug my system. Later I decided to go on my horse ride around the side of the house where the shocker was still in action. Old Blaze was soon dancing a jig all around the lawn. I think she sought and gained revenge by running under the low limb of the apple tree and dismounting me the next time I rode her in our back pasture.

One day Dad corralled our Hereford cattle in the wing of the barn and tried to catch one with a rope for some purpose. He had closed the exit with a board-paneled gate. After the second time the cattle broke through the gate, I offered to sacrifice my life for Dad's cause since nothing else seemed to be working. I got a significant wooden club in each hand. When the cattle began to come toward me at the exit, I whooped, screamed, and whacked as needed to turn them back. At the very moment of me nearly losing my nerve, Dad accomplished his purpose and the battle was won. I was proud as could be when Dad told Mom how "Reg outperformed a wooden gate!" (I guess that was better than being called "Dumber than a post").

We had great snow adventures. We found an old pointed car hood and dragged it to the steep hill at the farm where we propped up the nose of it with boards and packed it with snow. This made for an interesting ski jump. We hiked well above the jump, strapped on our old bear-trap bindings, and aimed for the car hood, which sent us shooting into the air.

In my teen years, Ron got a part-time job as the ranger for the Fairview snowmobile area. The state provided him a machine, which left his personal one for my use. I often patrolled with him up and down and all around and realized that the serious flaw in the system was that there was no one to patrol the ranger—he was a crazy man on snow. We should have perished in collision or avalanche, but the good ol' guardian angel was on duty and we survived. The worst accident we had was when I drove over a jump with my dad riding behind me, causing him to bruise his tailbone as he landed back on the machine. He healed in time and I think forgave me, but we did have to cancel our pending holiday trip to Idaho to visit Lowell and Louise.[40]

Some of my closest calls with death or disability came from my summer employment with the Hansen Lumber Company. One day I was working alone in the timber and had almost completed my final cut to fell a large tree when the wind shifted and pressed the tree opposite of where I wanted it to go, pinching my saw blade in the process. I tried inserting a series of wedges to move the tree in the right direction, but to no avail. I knew that if the wind would just blow in the opposite direction, the tree would move—but it didn't. As it was near the end of the day and we rarely ever saw anyone in our area, I left things in place and went home. I did not sleep well, imagining a sheepherder or someone riding by at the moment that the tree would fall. When I got to work the next morning, I gratefully found the tree flat on the ground with no sheepherder.

On another day, I was pushing a large log with the bulldozer when the log got perpendicular with an old, fallen tree covered with vegetation. My log got away and began rolling on the old tree down the hill toward the loading dock—which would not have been too concerning, except that as I looked in that direction, I discovered that Larry had just backed the log truck into the dock and was getting out. Thank you, angel, for stopping the log just before it got to Larry and his truck.

A few years previous to my work for Hansen Lumber, I had hitchhiked to Fairview Lakes to fish and then caught a ride home in the evening with Kent Miner, a local coal supplier. In our long, slow descent of Fairview Canyon, Kent startled me. In what was apparently a common trick for him to stay awake and get some exercise, he opened the door of the truck while it was still moving, climbed to the ground and ran alongside for a while, reaching his right arm to the steering wheel to hold the truck on course. A few years later as I was driving a load of logs down the canyon for Hansen Lumber, I thought, "Well, it worked for Kent so maybe it will work for me." I followed his example. I only did this one time because it dawned on me that I was not as skilled in the procedure as Kent likely was.

I purchased my first car—an old 1951 Ford with a plastic sun roof—from Worth Bench. I drove this car up and down the canyon road many times. My tires were generally bald and I often tried to straighten out the curves in the road by ignoring the yellow striping down the center. One night as I started down the canyon in the dark, smoke started pouring out of the dashboard. In my teenage wisdom, I reasoned that my chances of figuring out what was happening would be greater in our lighted yard at home rather than stuck in the dark canyon, so I rolled my windows down and stuck my head out for air and better sight. Luckily, I made it home and the burning stopped. I was never able to determine the source of the burning, but the car still worked, mostly, so I gave it no more thought.

Quite often as I worked for Hansen Lumber, I worked with Uncle Keith in the sawmill. I do not remember him ever training me in this stunt, but when I sensed that he might appreciate some help loading and turning the logs into sawing position, I mounted the log carriage and rode it from my station on the receiving end past the huge spinning saw blade to the loading area. I would help position the logs and would then ride the carriage back to my task. Since Uncle Keith did not stop me, I assumed the action was safe. I imagine that in any such sawmill today, there would be safety barriers preventing this action.

In more recent years, I have often imagined that deadly, ferocious saw blade and considered what might have happened had I caught a shoelace or lost my footing even once as I passed within inches of it. When I hear the antics of my children and grandchildren and counsel them in matters of safety, they sometimes say, "Did you ever do anything dangerous?" The conversation then fades into irrelevance. I pray for their protection and I hope my childhood guardian angel was retired with a full pension and plenty of peace and serenity.

Chapter Twenty-One:
A Working Fool

When Mom once told someone "Reg is a working fool!" I beamed with pride and was motivated to work even harder. But now in retrospect, I wonder if her emphasis was perhaps more on "fool." I am not sure. I suspect that whatever my ailment, it is genetic. I suppose if I could live life over again, there would be things I would change. I would like to have cultured more friendships—but I have many. I think I would have tried to diversify and explore my talents—but I am told I do have some, even though I do not sing or play a musical instrument. I think I would have tried to focus more of my energy toward sports, just in case I had a hidden aptitude. Now that I am retired, I am seeking new talents. Just this morning I made my first attempt at carving a swan out of an apple, and even though it perhaps looked more like an injured duck out of applesauce, I believe that I will do better tomorrow when I try again. When my little ones come to visit, I am fairly confident that I can surprise them with an apple-swan that looks too pretty to eat, but will encourage them to eat it anyway. Still, if I had to go back (which I am glad I do not have to do), I would try not to be quite such a fool about work.

I am actually very grateful for the principle of work and for the example of my parents who involved me in so many things from a young age. Some of my earliest memories are of gathering eggs from our chicken coop or bottle-feeding the baby lambs. As soon as I could churn the butter, the job was mine. I soon grew into the tasks of feeding the cows or sheep. I learned to care for my horse. I have early memories of riding on the dump rake to trip the handle as we raked the hay, or riding on the grain drill and poking the distribution tubes with a stick to keep them flowing. Once my size and strength accommodated carrying buckets of coal for the furnace, that became my responsibility.

Coal carrying—now there is an interesting commentary on parenting. Our home was heated by a coal furnace fed from a "stoker," or coal storage bin, with an auger that transferred the "slack," or small rocks of coal, from the stoker to the furnace. During the cold months, the furnace would consume several large steel buckets of coal each day. Dad had cleverly constructed a coal shed way out behind the barn, complete with a roof made of two huge hinged doors that could be propped open for the coal delivery truck to dump the coal directly into the shed. From that point forward, carrying the coal into the basement of the house and carrying the "clinkers," or residue from the burned coal, out to the back yard was where I came in. When I neglected my duty, the furnace ran out of coal and began to smoke. Each spring, Mom would have me help her clean the wallpaper with a gum-like substance that we used as scrubber. I soon learned that if I always kept the stoker full, there would not be so much cleaning in the spring.

I was fascinated with Dad's genius—as soon as I left home, he tore down the old coal shed and used the lumber elsewhere. He converted a basement fruit room into a convenient coal storage bin from which he could simply shovel the coal directly into the stoker just a few feet away. I marveled as to why it took so many years to think of this. I never thought of it—I just felt that it was my eternal destiny to carry coal.

I was fairly young when I discovered the world of free enterprise. I sold greeting cards all around town and soon had a base of repeat customers. I have to admit that I too often opted for the junk rewards offered in the catalog rather than the cash payments, but I soon figured it out. I collected and redeemed pop bottles and soon developed a clientele of folks who would give me their used bottles. I harvested and sold night crawlers to the fishermen, as I've mentioned. Norma helped me make a nice sign with a comical worm painted on it that I hung in the front yard so everyone who passed on Main Street would see it. I convinced some folks to give me their deer hides during hunting season, which I sold for a few dollars to Ted Barton, who was in that business. I contracted to deliver the morning edition of the *Salt Lake Tribune* around town, which I did for several years. For a few of those years, I also delivered the evening *Deseret News*, and through it all, Dad drove me—or let me drive—to deliver a Sunday edition through Oak Creek and Milburn. Floyd Young occasionally hired me to deliver promotional flyers for his drug store to every residence in town. For several years, I planned and grew my own garden—at least that was my intent. I think my folks probably did more of the weeding than I did, but it was a good project for a young boy to be involved in.

The very first hourly wage job I got was when a retired army officer named Ray Nielsen hired me to help Dad remodel a home Ray and his wife purchased just north of town. I was paid fifty cents an hour and spent my time in such activities as mixing plaster in a mud box, sanding the wooden porch columns, or just being a "gopher" for Dad.

A coal supplier occasionally hired me to help him unload in tight spots. My job was to get into the coal bin and shovel the coal evenly around as he unloaded it to me with an auger. As the bin filled to the top, I would lay down flat on the coal and move it around as best I could, leaving myself just barely enough room to exit. Mom said I came out "dirtier than a coal miner," and she convinced me that laundering my clothes was hardly worth the few dollars I was paid.

Through all my time working for others, we always had our own little farm to manage. Dad and I moved sprinkler pipe, hauled rocks, plowed, planted, harvested, cared for our animals, shoveled manure, built and repaired fences, maintained our machinery, and did all that was needed to keep our farm operating.

One day I went into Floyd Young's drug store to buy something and before I left, he had convinced me to come work for him. I did not really want to—I was making more money working for the local farmers by then—but he was kind of gruff and persuasive and before I knew it, I was a part-time soda jerk/cashier. Floyd taught me many things about sales and marketing. After I had worked for him for a time, he tried to persuade me to go to pharmacy school and come back and buy the place someday, but the thought never captured my heart.

I worked many day jobs for local farmers—mostly hauling hay for Stanley Brady, Reed Cheney, and Henry Wheeler. I worked more regularly for Kirby Bench milking cows, hauling manure, shoveling grain, hauling hay, mowing hay, and trying to keep the equipment in repair.

I spent the bulk of my mid-teens work time working for Turpin Dairy. I enjoyed working for and with the Turpins, my "cousins who were not my cousins" and "my uncle who was not my uncle." But I always felt like part of their family and they treated me as such. I worked mostly with Kevin, and later some with Wayne. Robyn drove the tractor for us as we hauled hay. Aunt Fern cooked lunch for us. Uncle Clarence was mostly working at the coal mine during the time that I worked on the dairy. I sometimes helped with cow milking, but mostly I built fences, hauled hay and manure, bailed hay, drove a truck as we chopped the corn, plowed with the big tractor, worked the silage pit, and did whatever else they found for me to do.

I consider my work for the Turpins some of the greatest foundational times of my life—I worked hard and learned self-confidence from the work they entrusted to me. Even after my mission and occasionally after my marriage, I returned and worked for them. Dad and I helped them with the construction of their new dairy barn. I remember how proud I was when they gave me the task of laying a concrete block wall around the oval-shaped milk tank. I added brick mason to my résumé, though no legitimate mason would have acknowledged my work. After my marriage, during my student teaching in Granite School District, the district teachers went on strike and stayed out for multiple weeks. We went to Fairview during the strike and stayed with my folks while I worked for the Turpins, mostly in the fall corn harvest. Each evening I watched the news to see if the strike had settled, and when it had not, I went to work the next day for the Turpins.

In my teen years, in the late afternoon of a hot summer day, Kevin and I were hauling hay in the south field and noticed three men walking toward us. I hoped that perhaps they were the Three Nephites coming to rescue us from our labors. But they were just the city fathers and they had come to talk to me. There would be a burial in the cemetery the next day and the only backhoe in town had broken down and would not be repaired in time to dig the grave. They had come to ask if I would hand-dig the grave. They told me that they knew that if I said I would do it, it would get done (Whoever said "flattery will get you nowhere" was wrong—at least it worked on me on this occasion). I left the hay field, got our pick and shovel, and met them in the cemetery where they had marked out the grave. They told me that the concrete vault was scheduled for delivery at eight o'clock the next morning and left me to my labors. They did not tell me about the hardpan composition of the soil.

The first foot or so of digging away the topsoil was relatively easy. Then things got hard. I had to figure out a system of shaving away a thin area of the heavily packed dirt to a certain depth, work my way back and forth, and then begin again at a new level. When darkness came, I was disheartened with my progress but went home to get a good night's sleep so I could be back at first light. When I found that I could not sleep thinking of that vault delivery truck arriving to a partial grave, I got up, dressed, and went back to the cemetery. After working through the night by light from my car headlights, I got the grave *almost* to the desired level as the vault truck arrived. From this experience, I learned that the cliché of "six feet under" could be applied as a rather subjective concept. I do not recall who the deceased was on this occasion, but hope I did not adversely affect his resurrection by only having him five feet and a few inches in the ground. As I never heard from him, I did not worry much about it.

After the dedication of the grave, I emerged from the outskirts of the cemetery, hand-filled the grave, and arranged the flowers on the mound. For my total work, Fairview City gave me thirty dollars, a huge "thank you," and assurance that I was now the city sexton. I probably dug nearly a half dozen graves total that summer. At the time of the start of school in the fall, I got notice to go dig the grave for Doc Rigby who had been tragically killed in an auto collision in Mt. Pleasant.

After digging to a significant depth, I struck something harder than the normal difficult soil and soon realized that I had encroached upon the final resting spot of old Doc Rigby, the father of the Doc I was supposed to be burying (In my defense, I was not in charge of engineering, just digging). With this new challenge, the city fathers had to employ a backhoe from a neighboring community to do a bit of rezoning to accommodate all parties. As I was now back in school, I relinquished my job as sexton to Uncle Jack, who I believe worked the assignment for some years thereafter.[41]

For the final two summers of my teens—one before my army basic training and one after—I worked for the Hansen Lumber Company with Jerry, Larry, and Uncle Keith—"my cousins who were my cousins" and my "uncle who was my uncle." Aunt Ruby Hansen and my mother are sisters. Uncle Keith was serving simultaneously as ward bishop and town mayor.

I was first put to work up in the mountains cutting timber with Jerry. He was significantly older and was well experienced in his craft. He was rather quiet, but he instructed me as needed. As we got better acquainted, I gained more appreciation and respect for him. I have often commented that he is one of the heroes of my youth.[42] At lunchtime, we would sit in the shade and listen to Paul Harvey news and talk about life. He often stayed overnight in a small trailer house near our work area. I often camped someplace, sleeping under the stars. Generally, I drove home and then back the next day. On a few occasions, I drove a log truck back and forth.

Jerry taught me how to maintain and operate a chain saw; how to fell, trim, and buck trees; how to skid logs with the small bulldozer; how to load the logs for transport; and how to clean up and pile the debris for future burning. This was a challenging time for Jerry in his life and sometimes he was absent. On those days, I worked alone and processed the value of being trustworthy to my employment without supervision.

I later coined a motto in expression of a philosophy—"there were no cheerleaders or cheering crowds deep in the timber," meaning that we learned to work without external recognition or accolade (Mostly, I think I was trying to compensate for my lack of athletic ability by seeking validation of my other abilities—which I came to accept as a legitimate life position).[43]

I did not get to work as much with Larry, who spent most of his time in home construction or driving the log truck. I did spend a few days with him in framing some homes, but my skills in that area were limited. But I was grateful for what I observed, especially many years later when I built my own home.

On many days, I worked in town with Uncle Keith in the sawmill. He occasionally sent me with a truck load of lumber for delivery, but mostly I was his helper in the mill (where he tried to work me to death). Years later when I had my little boys with me, we passed the mill and heard the saw going, so I pulled in and took them to see where I used to work. I could not resist pointing out to them that Uncle Keith and a couple of men were doing what he and I used to do by ourselves. But in all fairness, he was older then and perhaps labor laws had caught up with him or something.

Nevertheless, he was quite amazing. When I heard the roar of the saw as he turned it on, I knew we were in for a wild ride. He worked like a madman, it seemed. My job was to receive the fresh-sawn lumber, sort and stack it appropriately, keep the sawdust auger and pile clear and working, stack the slabs, and help him on his end of the carriage in getting the logs from the dock into sawing position. Just when I thought I would collapse from fatigue or get buried by lumber, slabs, or sawdust, a loud bell would ring and he would turn off the saw. The bell was his telephone in the office, so off he would go to discuss mayor or bishop business. At those times, I realized how grateful I was for his community service and his calling and how busy they kept him. I would have a chance to get things sorted out and almost have a bit of a rest break, but then the saw would begin to whir once again and off we would go.

After working my first summer in the mill and the timber, I left for army basic training. Yes, it was demanding—emotionally, spiritually, culturally, and physically. But as we sat around so much of the time while the smokers smoked and the whiners whined, I often considered how nice it was to finally have a rest.

Chapter Twenty-Two:
The Falcons and the Hawks

As I write this, I am at my home in Wisconsin as a red-tailed hawk perched in our backyard maple tree is devouring a critter and scattering the leftovers on the snow-covered ground near our garden shed. I suppose the falcon and the hawk were fitting mascots for our junior high and high school—the sports guys always seemed to want to devour and scatter their opponents. I worried that junior high and high school would devour and scatter me all around. It was a hard thing to board the big yellow school bus and drive the thirty-mile round trip to Moroni after spending the first dozen years of my life in my sheltered and familiar hometown. There were strangers there and some of them even said bad words and smoked cigarettes (Oh my!). But I soon met people who would become my lifelong friends and for whom I am eternally grateful. I guess that is a metaphor for life—we need to dare to exit our zones of comfort if we want to learn to live comfortably in a larger realm.

In an effort to prompt my memory of these times, I did a systematic search of my junior high and high school yearbooks. My, what memories, and what an interesting foretelling of life. For example, Brent and Sally, two years older than me, were a couple way back when I was in seventh grade. Just a few days ago on Facebook, I saw that they recently returned from a mission in New England, nearly a half-century later. David and Eddi, a couple from high school days, are, with their son, currently in Hawaii serving a mission. I name these folks as just a sample of so many who have inspired me to do better and look higher. I sense the hazards of naming only a few, because there were so many good folks. I hope someday in a more eternal realm I can reconnect with all of them and see how our lives have been blessed by association.

Riding the bus was a new, scary, and exciting adventure. I was quite amazed at the intrigue of positioning for the very back seats—battles were sometimes fought over them. I later considered the strange irony of the battles fought at the same time in the Deep South in quest of the front seats on the bus. Ferg was our driver, and he seemed a kindly man who generally kept his cool. I recall one day when a wheel came off an oncoming vehicle, rolled toward us, and smacked us square in the front bumper and hood. No harm was done except to the bus. Another day, someone from an ongoing car threw a peach head-on at our bus and broke our windshield. We maintained a certain loyalty to our bus and driver, even making up a little parody of another bus driver who was known for his extra caution. It was sung to the tune of the old US Army song "The Army Goes Rolling Along." The words went something like "Over hill, over dell, as he hits the asphalt trail . . . For it's hi-hi-hee when he's going over three [implying his speed] . . . And we think he's great when he's going over eight . . ." and so forth.

I soon became acquainted with people who, in addition to my Fairview friends, would be my lifelong friends—Mel, Dave, Mark, George, Tom, Carl, Jerry, and Hal, to offer a sampling. I have often wondered if they were nervous and self-conscious like me. They did not seem to be, but I have learned that we don't often see another's fears very well. But they had perspective and self-confidence. For example, one day my friend Carl and I were outside during lunchtime when the breeze shifted and brought that familiar, awful stench our way from the by-product burnings of the turkey processing plant. I said, "Carl, how can you stand to live in this town?" His dad and his uncles were successful turkey growers. He took a long, deliberate inhale of the fowl air (pun intended) and then simply said, "Ah, money!" He made his point, but I was still glad to breathe the fresh Fairview air at the end of the day.

The teachers were sincere and dedicated to their charge. I had English from Helen Madsen and felt a connection with her when I learned that as a young lady, she had gone horseback riding with my mother. Spud Anderson taught shop and crafts (His real name was "Hugh," which we sometimes mispronounced as "Huge"—so either way, it reflected his physique). He gained my lifelong respect when, during my time of a rather extended illness, he made house calls to check on me and bring me homework projects to do. He also called me out in class one time to compliment me on doing the work he had brought me. I have already mentioned Jerry Nelson, our coach, who seemed to keep a special watch on us even after our baseball careers ended. It was good to see him at school each day. Red-headed Phillip Johnson took over as shop teacher when Spud retired. We called him "carrot top"—but only once, as I recall. He helped me build my showcase and was very good to me.

Bruce Irons was our PE coach and health teacher and had a system of fines for violation of class rules. At the semester end, I remember that he sent me and a few others with the money collected to town to buy junk food for a class party (We learned that the more rules we broke, the bigger the party). Max Blain was a great artist and tried hard to help me become one—but to no avail. But his son-in-law Mack Wilkey did help me learn some commercial art skills in high school. Vaughn Madsen had my interest because, like me, he loved to fish, and he was also in our bishopric. I felt sorry for Otis Nielsen who was dying of cancer while trying to hang on to his teaching job. I do not think I had a class from him, but he was my neighbor and also my bishop when I was very young. My eighth-grade yearbook has a nice "In Memory" tribute to him in commendation of his thirty-eight years as an educator.

Marsden Allred taught band and seemed kind of gruff—especially when, on the bus ride to march in the Strawberry Days parade in Pleasant Grove, the bass drummer deliberately poked the handle of his mallet through the drum head so he would not have to march in the parade. As I nervously faded into the background for my year or so in band, Mr. Allred never really discovered that I had not mastered my instrument or the concept of music generally. A great irony here is that I did gain appreciation for music, even though I could not play it, and went on to later write a commentary on Handel's *Messiah*.[44]

"Prophet" George Anderson was our seminary teacher in our small seminary building located between the main building and the gymnasium. He was a great man and the father of my friend Mark. His wife taught home economics at our school. In my particular class, there were only a half-dozen or so boys and no girls. Brother Anderson had assigned us to quietly read one day and in the silence, we heard the wind begin to blow. Woody slammed his big fist on the desk and blurted out loud, "Hot damn, I am going to go home and fly my kite!" On another occasion, Woody came at me on the basketball floor ready to beat me up. I must have fouled him or stolen the ball or something; I did not really know what I had done. Anyway, I tried real hard to apply what Prophet had taught us about being peacemakers. Also, I realized that fighting a boy with one arm would be a "lose-lose." If you "win," you are a coward for taking advantage. I also knew that if I "lost," if he were to hit me with that powerful arm, he would knock me clear back to Fairview. So I shook his hand and apologized for whatever I had done. I think we were pretty good friends after that.

I really enjoyed the activities provided for us. In the fall, if we could persuade our teachers to grant permission, we were allowed to go to the auditorium as a class and watch the World Series. My friend and I used an old pair of my Dad's overalls and constructed a dummy for the Halloween party. We thought we were cool. We had several lyceum assemblies where we were introduced to singers, dancers, magicians, and scientists. I recall an incident that demonstrates my complete naïveté at that young age. Some black men had performed for us and then they came to the lunch room to eat with us. They sat at my table and I got to visit with them. I went to my class after lunch and informed my friends that I knew that "they were not real blacks because the palms of their hands were white." I had so much to learn. The culture and diversity of the world seemed so far removed.

I would not, of my own awareness, have anticipated anything unusual or even recognized the historic significance of February 9, 1964, had it not been for the before-and-after giddy chatter and growing excitement of the girls on our bus and in our classes. On that Sunday evening of my seventh grade year, a new musical group from Great Britain made their first TV appearance in the United States performing on the *Ed Sullivan Show*. They called themselves The Beatles. My old-school Tucker uncles—who had some musical talent—called them "a bunch of long-haired spoiled brats who could not carry a tune in a coal bucket." However people perceived them, they were here to stay and, like it or not, this would be the beginning of what has become known as the "British Invasion" of countless musical groups who would turn the changing world upside down.

My world was changing. I discovered that my friendships did not need to be restricted to boys. One girl flirted with me and teased me a bit, giving me the nickname of "Lurch" because I was tall like the butler on the TV show *The Addams Family* (The nickname did not stick, but I think I liked the fact that a girl had given it to me). We had some school dances. My sister, Norma, instructed me in basic etiquette and dance. Even Uncle Ralph took time to teach me how to dance the popular new "Twist"—"Just pretend that you are drying your back with a towel that you are holding with both hands and moving back and forth. Now while doing that, spread your feet apart and pretend that you are extinguishing two cigarette butts—one under each foot." It worked—that was exactly what it looked like to me. I did not think that even Chubby Checker could do it better.

I began to look forward to the occasional matinee dances held during school hours. I even spruced up and rode the bus to the school on the occasion of our few special night dances. One girl recalled to me a few years later how I had danced with her at the junior high dance. She remembered the name of the song and the exact description of what she was wearing and what I said and a whole bunch of other stuff that had not registered with me. I have since wondered if, in my shyness, I would have ever mustered the courage to ask a girl for a date if she had not invited me to go to the high school girl's-choice preference ball with her a few years later.

High school had some definite advantages. For one, the bus ride was only twelve miles round trip, plus I would soon be driving my own car so I could come and go as I pleased. We seemed to have more freedom—we felt we had escaped from "Hillcatraz," as we had affectionately called our junior high on the hill in Moroni. Life seemed more relaxed and we already had established friendships. I was still nervous about life, but I suppose all were to some degree or another.

I am grateful for my good friends. I think I tried to be friendly with most people and was grateful for their acceptance and encouragement of me. I was impressed that the older students accepted me and made me feel comfortable. There was evidence of alcohol and tobacco use off campus, but I do not recall any illegal drug challenges—perhaps I was just naïve. I remember expressing my total incredulity when a girl got pregnant, but my friend helped me better understand by stating that "it likely surprised them too." I soon fell in with the guys who were the school athletes, which seemed ironic since I had so little in common with them. But they accepted me and I was grateful for their example and their friendship.

We had good teachers and leaders. Kay Lay was a big and rather intimidating principal, but once I got acquainted with him, he seemed helpful and friendly to me. My neighbor Loa Cheney taught us English. Lawrence Kelson was a tough old bird who ran the farm mechanics shop with an iron fist and not much tolerance for horseplay. Elden Westenskow was old and tired and near retirement and spent most of our agriculture class in the teacher's lounge. But he was a good soul. Lowell Hansen taught us biology and threatened to expel us when we threw some of our dissected frogs from his third-floor classroom window. Harold Mickel worked so hard to teach geometry, algebra, and math—he really knew what he was talking about. The problem was that I did not know what he was talking about. I look back now with a philosophy that everyone kind of goes out into the world and adapts math concepts to the needs of their life and profession. That adaptation, plus the invention of the electronic calculator, saved me in my carpet business and my profession.

Brent Rock coached me in tennis, the only sport I played. Isabelle Johnson seemed so old, and she did retire soon after I got to high school—hopefully this was not a cause-and-effect scenario. As I got to know her in Spanish class, we got along fine. She once hosted a great social for our class in a Mexican restaurant in Fountain Green where we practiced our Spanish. I have already mentioned how Mack Wilkey blessed my life with principles of commercial art, which helped me immensely in my teaching profession. He also taught us how to drive, although he expressed surprise that I already seemed experienced when I got behind the wheel. I explained about my Sunday paper route and how Dad always let me drive.

Brothers Jim Carver and Ron Bradley inspired me in seminary. I think they, along with Brother Anderson in ninth grade, planted the seeds in my heart that would grow into my desire to follow in their professional footsteps. Plus, it seemed like good, clean, indoor work with no heavy lifting, and you got to hang out with good people in a good place all day and be involved in a good cause (After just completing thirty-seven years in this profession, I affirm that my early perceptions were fairly accurate—although there has been much more to it than I ever realized when I began).

Like most young people, when I got my driver's license at the beginning of my junior year, I felt I had arrived at maturity. I already had my own car by then, but it wasn't much. My brother Ron had a fancy car I could borrow for special occasions, and Dad even got a better car that was adequate for what I needed. I was blessed. Now that I was sixteen and had a car, the next logical step was to begin dating. I honestly do not recall my thoughts and feelings about this transition, but I suppose I considered who I would invite and how I would go about it. But then, Marie, the girl who remembered the details of our junior high dance, invited me. I was pleased but very nervous. We seemed to get along well and continued dating—quite steadily for most of the rest of my time in high school. She had a good family and high standards, and as I consider those times of my life, I become more grateful for her and the example she set.

Near the end of my high school experience, I had the opportunity to date several other great girls and am also thankful for each and their good lives. In reviewing my yearbooks, I have pleasant thoughts about all of the pretty girls who said nice things. I am also pleased to read "Love ya" from some of the guys. It just meant friendship, for which I was grateful. In my senior year, I was elected as "most preferred man" by the girls' organization and honored at the preference ball (I suffered the same fate a few years later at Snow College). I think this came about because I opened doors for them, did not tease them too much, and tried to say hello to everyone—at least I would like to remember that I did.

I am not sure how I was persuaded to wear a dress (a kilt, specifically) and become a dancer in *Brigadoon*, our annual school play. I suppose Marie and her friends roped me into it as they needed partners. But it was fun to be part the production. I enjoyed other school activities, too—I think I participated in one traveling speech and drama meet. I recall one time when several of us put on a school assembly with an attempt to duplicate the popular TV comedy show *Laugh In*. My role was to feign a hurt leg and make it look serious so Mr. Wilkey would come to the stage and examine my injury. My punch line as he examined my leg was, "No, it is my arm!" (I guess you had to be there). We attended the ball games and celebrated when our little school won the state basketball championship in a David and Goliath matchup. The whole community went wild with excitement and I was happy for my friends who had found this success from their efforts on the team.

I did not get into too much mischief and only recall one occasion when my friends and I cut school for half a day or so and went on a long car ride. Mr. Lay, the principal, got word and was waiting for us upon our return. My memory of this occasion is of him just shaking his head at us and scolding, "Look at you. You are the leaders of the school and are supposed to be examples to others. Just what am I supposed to do with you?" I guess he never figured it out, because he just turned and walked off and nothing more came of the matter.

Since our FFA (Future Farmers of America) class was left alone most of the time without a teacher, we turned it into a study hall/goof-off period. We governed ourselves with our own "board of education"—a large wooden paddle drilled full of holes. When one of us offended our code of decency, we had to stand and lean over a table while another appointed to mete out our punishment would give us a good whack. I received a few, which was a few too many for my liking.

I am not sure how I got appointed or elected to be the president of the FFA my senior year. I was not planning to be a farmer and did not even have an active project at that time. We were well into the laundry business by then. But I served as a delegate to the state convention and organized our annual FFA ball. I served on the student council to provide leadership and activities for the student body. I also went to the national convention, teaming up with other delegates from across the state for our long train ride to Kansas City. I recall meeting my three roommates, all from the same rural Utah high school. I was the lone wolf. I assumed we would walk over to the convention together, but as soon as we checked into our room, they announced that they were going to do some drinking and go to the burlesque shows. I am not sure how successful they were in their quest, but I never saw much more of them.

I went to the convention center and listened to a variety of speakers who talked about the economic outlook, innovations, and the future of farming. Our largest crowd showed up for a speaker I had heard of but had not paid much mind to before—Richard Nixon. I have tried to recall if he gave his emotional plea "I am not a crook" then, or if he said that some other time. He was staying at our hotel, and when I went back, I could not get in for quite a while due to heightened security. I finally entered a back laundry door and found my way to our room. A few weeks later, Richard Nixon was elected as President of the United States.[45]

I still had no plans to be a farmer, but my experiences began my thought processes about a future career. I considered dairy processing and even expressed this to our teacher and advisor, Mr. Westenskow. He said he would gladly arrange a tour for me at Utah State University in Logan. In this pre-GPS era, I expressed nervousness to him about finding my way to Logan as I had never been there before. He drew me a map and assured me all would be fine and that I would see signs pointing me to Logan. When the day came, I drove Dad's big Chrysler with three other boys who were interested in the trip. When we got to Logan and reported to the professor who was to show us around, he knew nothing of our planned visit—Mr. W. had failed to contact him. But he graciously arranged a tour for us of the dairy processing plant, the breeding facility, and the meat packing operation nearby. We had an informative and interesting day.

When we returned to class the next day, Mr. W. had remembered what he was supposed to do and was very apologetic. I assured him that all was fine—that I had driven up the freeway just past Salt Lake and exited when we saw the sign "Lagoon," just like he said we should. I told him we had a great day riding the roller coasters and playing the games.

As my high school years were coming to a close, I reflected on what my teachers and classmates thought of me and where I would go next in life. I had always looked in awe and admiration at those who were class valedictorians or voted "most likely to succeed." I was never a candidate for either honor. I was voted the wittiest—basically a euphemism for being a smart aleck. I could relate to that. When old Arthur B. one morning many years before scolded me for not having his newspaper to his house as early as he wanted it, I had said "Mr. B., why don't you go down to Carlson's Grocery and sit on the end of the counter so everyone will know that you are the Big Cheese?" My friend reminds me that I once told him of a special feature on my old Ford called a "magnetic rear end." When he inquired of its purpose, I said, "To catch all the junk that falls off the front end." These, of course, were just recycled witticisms I had probably picked up from TV. Now that I had the official title of wittiest, I soon grew into my own original sense of wit.

I once heard a definition of *wit* as something like "the ability to eliminate the thirty-second delay period between when you hear a comment and when you think of a clever retort or action to the comment." One of my classic missed opportunities involved an apostate whom I will call Bob. He lived in my ward boundaries when I was bishop, but he had left the church years before. He still presented himself to people as an active church member, and when he met me, he always derisively asked when he could come in and get his temple recommend. One day, I went to transact some business in the city office and Bob was there flirting with (or better said, harassing) the office ladies. When he saw me, he made a loud pretense of saying, "Oh Bishop Christensen, so good to see you. When may I come in and get my temple recommend?" I gave him a quiet and direct "Not this year," or something. I have regretted not turning to the ladies in mock astonishment and saying, "Pardon me, ladies, but I have been out of town for a week or so. Did hell happen to freeze over while I was gone?"

Some of my favorite wit comes when I have ample time to plan and ponder. One day our military unit was at Camp Williams involved in mock war. First Sergeant Chesley Christensen could not attend and assigned me to represent him. My job was to manage the supply of our troops— all on paper, of course. I got a written request, "Needed: twelve shovels, ASAP." I pondered and then replied, "Shovels back-ordered 24 hours. In the meantime, just lean on each other." On another occasion during my army basic training in Missouri, we were seated in a mid-afternoon classroom instruction after a rigorous and tiring morning of training. A trick the instructors used to keep us awake was to pause mid-sentence and yell the command "On your feet!" at which we were to all jump to attention. One day my buddy Ervin just could not keep his eyes open and his chin off his chest. 1 plotted for just the right moment and then carefully leaned over and nudged him with my elbow, whispering in his ear, "Ervin, on your feet!" He jumped to attention, only to look around and realize that he was the only person standing. It was grand, and the instructor was good natured about it and gave Ervin a good teasing.

Wit is particularly rewarding when it is spontaneous and perfectly timed. One day I was installing new carpeting in a complicated family room in Orem. The homeowner was watching me as I speedily made my cuts to allow the new carpet to lie around the fireplace hearth and other deviations to the square room. He did not understand that these were just rough cuts—more exact cutting and seaming would come later and with more time for planning and precision. He said, "Wow, doesn't that scare you to cut like that?" I replied, "Why would it scare me? It's your carpet."

On the first day back to school after Thanksgiving break, I was visiting with my seminary students as they entered my classroom. Doug was a good, likeable boy but had some social struggles. As he entered, I said, "Hey, Doug, how was your Thanksgiving?" He patted his stomach and replied, "Boy, was I stuffed!" Quick as a flash, in vintage wit, I said, "Well, Doug, most turkeys were." I'm not sure how Doug felt, but he looked embarrassed as everyone laughed.

I believe that the value of education is not just to prepare us to make a living—we do much of that on the job after we get the key to open desired doors—but to teach us how to live peaceably and respectfully with all people. By this definition, I conclude that I received a great education at the hands of diligent teachers and cherished friends. So many people modeled for me the importance of not tearing people apart and scattering them around, but encouraging and uplifting and loving no matter the circumstance or station in life. As I look back in retrospect of my life, if I had it to do over again, I would not have insulted Mr. B. with my "Big Cheese" comment. I am grateful now that my wit did not kick in as I had wished it did with Bob in the city office. I for sure would have still nudged Ervin in the ribs, retorted as I did to the man about his carpet, and responded the same to the soldiers about the shovels.

What about Doug? I made a commitment to myself that day that I have tried hard to keep—when there is potential to inflict harm or embarrassment, I need to not be so danged witty.

Chapter Twenty-Three:

A President is Slain

I suppose most of us recall where we were and what we were doing when we heard news of great consequence. On July 20, 1969, I watched the TV footage of Astronaut Neil Armstrong as he descended from the Apollo 11 space craft onto the surface of the moon and said, "That's one small step for a man; one giant leap for mankind."[46] On Tuesday, September 11, 2001, I had visited one of my early morning seminary teachers in her class and was en route to a university a few hours away to teach an institute class. I had stopped to have breakfast at Cracker Barrel in Madison when my wife called to tell me that an airplane had just flown into one of the twin trade towers in New York.

In the fall of 1963, I had just turned twelve and started junior high school as a seventh grader. On Friday, November 22, I was home ill from school and was watching TV when our programs were interrupted just after noon (CST) with the news that President John F. Kennedy had been shot in Dallas, Texas. For the next several days, we stayed tuned to what was my, and I suppose most people's, first experience with around-the-clock news coverage. I was seeking answers to my many questions. This was such a shocking and terrible thing. How could someone just shoot and kill the president of the United States? How badly was he wounded? Would he live? If he died, then what? Who would be the new president and how would he be appointed? Who did this terrible thing? Would they find the person? Was he acting alone? My questions multiplied as I looked to such reporters as Walter Cronkite, Dan Rather, Chet Huntley, and David Brinkley for answers.

From the subsequent news coverage, we learned that President and Mrs. Kennedy had landed within the hour in Dallas at Love Field and were en route to the Dallas Business Trade Mart where the president was to give a luncheon speech. They rode in the second car in the presidential motorcade—a 1961 Lincoln Continental with the bubbletop open. The front seat was occupied by a Secret Service agent (the driver) and the president's bodyguard, the center seat by Texas Governor John

Connally and Mrs. Connally. First Lady Jacqueline Kennedy was in the left rear seat and the president was in the right rear seat. The motorcade had stopped along the way for the president to shake hands with some Catholic nuns and then again to greet some schoolchildren.

Just before 12:30 p.m., the presidential limousine made a sharp left-hand turn from Houston onto Elm Street and was slowly approaching the Texas School Book Depository. Shots were heard just after the President had started waving with his right hand. President Kennedy, with a shocked expression and mouth open, clenched his fists, raised his arms in front of his face, and leaned toward Mrs. Kennedy. The president then received another shot to his head. Mrs. Kennedy screamed and began to climb out of the back seat and onto the rear of the limo. Secret Service Agent Clint Hill climbed onto the rear of the limo and Mrs. Kennedy returned to the seat. The limo driver and police motorcycles sped up and headed for Parkland Hospital.[47]

At Parkland Hospital, a Roman Catholic priest administered last rites for President Kennedy and he was pronounced dead at 1:00 p.m. Vice President Lyndon Johnson, not knowing the extent of the situation and perhaps wondering if it were the result of a larger conspiracy, requested that the death announcement not be made until after they left the hospital to go to Air Force One. Shortly after 2:00 p.m., the body of President Kennedy was removed from Parkland Hospital and transported to Air Force One. Once Mrs. Kennedy and the president's body were back on Air Force One, Lyndon Johnson was sworn in as the thirty-sixth president of the United States of America at 2:38 p.m. They arrived back in Washington, DC, at approximately 6:00 p.m (EST). Mrs. Kennedy refused to leave the body of her husband that evening and into the early hours of the morning. She also refused to change her blood stained dress, exclaiming, "I want them to see what they have done to Jack."

After the president was shot, Lee Harvey Oswald was confronted by a policeman in the Texas School Book Depository but was not detained when it was made known that he was an employee there. He exited the building and was later seen entering a theatre, after J.D. Tippitt, a police officer, had been shot and killed. Oswald was arrested in the theatre and was charged that evening with the murder of Officer Tippit. Just before midnight, he was also charged with the murder of President Kennedy. On Sunday, November 24, we had just returned from church and tuned our TV back to the continuing coverage when we learned that Lee Harvey Oswald had been shot and killed in police custody by Jack Ruby, a Dallas nightclub owner.

We continued to watch as events of the funeral unfolded. After autopsy and embalming, the president's body was taken Saturday afternoon to the East Room of the White House where it lay in repose in closed casket for twenty-four hours. A funeral mass was held Sunday morning. On Sunday afternoon, the body was transported by horse-drawn caisson to the Capitol Rotunda for public viewing of the casket lying in state through the evening and commencing the next morning. However, due to the large number of visitors—250,000 total—the lines were kept open all Sunday night. On Monday, the body was taken back to the White House and then on to St. Matthews Cathedral for the state funeral. One of my vivid memories is of the saddled riderless horse with empty riding boots turned backwards in the stirrups.

After the state funeral, the cortège proceeded to Arlington National Cemetery for burial. Just after descending the steps of the cathedral, Mrs. Kennedy leaned down and whispered to her son, John Jr., who offered an honorable salute to his father's casket. This was John Jr.'s third birthday. A photo of this sweet tribute from a young boy to his father became an icon of the times and remains one of my most vivid memories.

I do not remember anything about celebrating Thanksgiving a few days after President Kennedy's funeral. I am sure we did, but we had been so shocked by the events that I am certain we were distracted from our usual thoughts and feelings. I gained somewhat of a fascination for all things Kennedy—I have since read several biographies of the Kennedys and viewed many documentary presentations of their family history. My interest has been repeatedly kindled by the continuing drama of their family. A few years ago, I stopped to buy donuts for my institute class and happened to cross paths with the owner of a long-revered Madison business. He was a chatty guy and, when he realized that I was Mormon, seemed to delight in telling me the history of his store and of its previous owners who were Mormons. From there, he went on to tell how his building had once been owned by the Kennedy family and how the proceeds from the leases had been used for the care and keeping of President Kennedy's sister Rosemary who lived for years in a care facility in Wisconsin (That is another fascinating and sad Kennedy drama/tragedy that I won't go into here).

In my final year of high school, I exercised my Kennedy fascination by choosing the president's assassination as the topic of my senior research project for our English class. In searching memorabilia, I actually found my old paper, "An American Tragedy: The Assassination of John Fitzgerald Kennedy." This was my first ever significant attempt to write something of substance. As I now read through it, I am a bit embarrassed by its flaws and formatting errors, but I console myself with the reminder that we did not have word processors with spell checkers in that time and place. I had only an old manual typewriter with a worn ribbon. When it came time to type the final draft, I remember asking my former home teaching companion Alt Jones if I could borrow his ward clerk's office at the church so I could have access to a better typewriter. He cleared it with the bishop, and they let me do so. I recall that I missed a day of school to complete this project. The next day, I proudly submitted my paper to Mrs. Cheney and wondered why I had not been invited to join the Warren Commission. But I did get an A- on the paper, so I was satisfied.

In my paper, I had basically followed the conclusions of the Warren Commission, but also discussed the notion of conspiracy theories. My concluding paragraph reads, "Although there is doubt as to who killed President John Fitzgerald Kennedy, the fact still remains that one of our greatest presidents is dead. He did much for the American people and will remain in our memory forever."

He sure remained in my memory. I was discussing the assassination last week with my brother-in-law who is reading a book about one of the alternate theories of the killing. This prompted me to share with him a six-hour video of a mock trial of Lee Harvey Oswald produced about thirty years ago. Before I shared the video, I watched it again myself—it was a poignant encounter with my memory of the events. Produced about twenty years after the assassination, many actual witnesses were interviewed and cross-examined in the mock trial. To again hear their testimonies of the events of these fateful days affirms some of my beliefs, but it also fosters some of my doubts about this great American tragedy. The defending attorney in the trial makes a good point that there is truth that is, in a sense, "locked in a closet," and we will not know the whole truth of the matter until the closet is unlocked.

Through it all, I have drawn the following conclusions:
1. Although I believed the Warren Commission report released in the fall of 1964, and I still lean in that direction, I have since heard many alternate theories, some of which are totally absurd. Others may have some elements of truth.
2. After watching the enhanced version of the Zapruder film, frame 313, I have no doubt that the President died instantly

from that gunshot and that there was no "brain" left to be stolen or hidden away somewhere as some may claim.

3. Although drudgery at the time, my high school research project was a great foundation stone of my life. It infused me with adequate doses of confidence and experience that have led me through a lifetime of researching and writing projects in college and in my profession, four volumes of my personal history, and five published books. Sometimes things that are difficult turn out to be good for us after all.

4. Although there are many things I do not know and many things I would like to know, I trust that I do know (or have opportunity to learn) all that I need to know at present and that all things that I would like to know will someday be given to me in due time and place. "Wherefore, the things of all nations shall be made known; yea, all things shall be made known unto the children of men."[48]

Chapter Twenty-Four:

The Supreme Love of Mama Skunk

As a boy, like countless boys through the years, I received a new Daisy Red Ryder BB gun for Christmas. Perhaps I was warned, "You'll shoot your eye out," but I do not recall.[49] I went on my first hunting expedition through the neighborhood and saw a little bird in a tree branch up against the windowless side of a neighbor's house. I shot and hit—the bird fell lifeless to the ground. I felt rather strange and was likely processing in my subconscious mind why I had done this peculiar thing.

Our garden here in Wisconsin is plagued with rabbits. My wife would like me to shoot them, but I always remind her that we live within the village limits and shooting would be illegal. Sometimes we discuss alternate methods of eliminating the rabbits, and when I run out of rational excuses, I fess up by openly reminding her that I am a conscientious objector about killing rabbits and other critters. I do not like to kill anything, period. I would rather build a fence.

How did I evolve from cold-blooded killer to tender-hearted pacifist? It is a long story, but I will try to be brief. Don't get me wrong—I believe that animals are for the use of mankind and I have no qualms with those who like to hunt. I understand that deer populations, for example, need management. I even laughed at the bumper sticker on the old pickup truck of Sarah Palin's father when she made her bid for vice president: "Vegetarian—Old Indian Word for Bad Hunter." I am neither exclusively vegetarian nor carnivore. I have friends who are vegetarian and even vegan and I am happy to dine with them on their menu or give them our extra zucchini. I also enjoy an occasional beef steak—I just prefer that someone else kill and process it. But, if I had to do so for sustenance, I would (and have done so).

One of my earliest memories was when I stood before the ward Christmas audience and recited my line, "The people set out a few sheaves of grain so the birds too could enjoy Christmas dinner." I was totally embarrassed that people laughed at me—but my mother put all things right by explaining that it was because I was so cute. I just know that I was speaking with heartfelt emotion—I was happy that the little birds were remembered and fed.

One day I found an old bird cage and announced to my family that I was going out to hunt for a bird to put in it. They just laughed. By strange luck, I had not gone far into our horse pasture when sure enough, I found my bird—a young sparrow that had apparently been displaced from its nest and had fallen into a hoof print in the soft mud. The bird, not knowing that I just wanted to protect it, nervously squawked and fluttered as I quickly secured it in my cage and took it back to my family. They were as surprised as I was delighted. I cared for the bird and protected it from harmful weather and predators until it could be set free once again.

I have sweet memories of nurturing the newborn lambs we placed in a box and brought into the house near the oven door for an incubation period. We raised our own chickens and I gathered the eggs from the layers and helped scald and pluck the meat birds after Dad had axed off their heads on the old tree stump.

As I grew older, I sometimes pulled the trigger in butchering for meat or mercy-killing, but preferred that Dad or my brothers perform this duty. One day, Ron and I were out at the barn near the San Pitch with the duty of slaughtering a hog. We were so clever—we had a container of food positioned right under the barn beam with a block-and-tackle all ready to go so we would not need to transport or do a manual lift. We attracted the unsuspecting victim into position and then Ron shot—and just missed his mark of death but still connected (This was very unusual for Ron, but this was in his younger days). The ensuing scene was chaotic before we accomplished our task.

When I worked for the Turpins, I think I noticed a tender heart in them for their livestock. After spending your time and energy in the care and keeping of animals, you develop a certain attachment and respect. I believe I sensed this and offered one day to put a sick cow out of its misery. They seemed grateful. I then buried it with the backhoe out in the far end of the lot.

Charlie and Ron were great fishers and hunters of pheasants, deer, and elk. I grew into their culture and imagined myself to someday be like them. They seemed to enjoy taking me fishing—I think, in retrospect, so I would clean all of the fish. I processed hundreds! I never hunted elk with them. I accompanied them on several deer hunts and remember two that got away. In thick trees, I saw the biggest buck I had ever seen and held my gun at the ready. When I got clear sight for a shot, Charlie was just beyond and nearly in line of my fire. I chose not to shoot, for which he later thanked me when I explained. On another early morning, I was on a drive out west when the second biggest buck I had ever seen came creeping up the draw towards me. After my shot rang through the hills, I had the embarrassing task of yelling to Ron that I had missed and it had gotten away (Since both of these deer got away, I can imagine them to be as big as I please). I later used the excuse that I had not slept much as I had been on the train from the FFA convention in Kansas City for a few days—which probably had some bearing on my missed shot, but not enough to justify it to my brothers.

I remember my excitement at shooting my first pheasant, and then my disappointment and embarrassment when I saw that it was a hen, and then my confusion and subsequent pride when Ron explained that it was not a hen, but rather a spring rooster. I felt at the time that I would just never catch on to this hunting stuff. Yet on a later occasion I was hunting alone after school through some tall cover near the San Pitch when the air just exploded with flying pheasants. I downed the first rooster that flew and then fumbled to reload my old single-shot twelve-gauge while several more escaped—but then I got one more. I found Ron at the Travel Inn and reported to him with pride, but it turns out that Blacky (Harold Blackburn), the game warden, had already told him about it after watching the whole show with his scope. I thought I had arrived. I think I was nearly as excited to get my hunting license as I was for my driver's license.

Dad did what he had to do to manage and process the farm animals, but I sensed that he had a reverence for life too. Once, when I was a young married guy and we had our ward members camping at our farm, there was a scraggly old one-eared mule with curled up hooves that had wandered into our property. Dad expressed that he should likely shoot it, but he just did not want to, so he had let it wander. We spent a few hours catching it, tied it in the trees for hiding, and then presented it as a gift of gratitude to my bishop at the evening campfire. Larry, a rough and tumble old cowboy with a tender heart—especially for animals—relieved the bishop of his quandary. Larry was proceeding to load the mule in his motorhome and haul it back to Lehi where he planned to care for it and restore it to health (except for the missing ear) when his wife stopped him. I think he came back later and got it with his truck. Larry broke down and sobbed one day during his testimony when he told of an injured cow that he had to part with. I sensed his pain.

I remember feeling sorry for the horses at the coal mine. To me they seemed overworked. As I observed how one old farmer undernourished his cows, I felt sad and frustrated. When I was young and married, we stayed at my folks' home and cared for the animals while they were on an extended visit to Norma in Chicago. One of the calves seemed sickly and soon died—and then another and another. I hauled one to Moroni to Doc Ramsey and he diagnosed it as quick pneumonia and helped me save the few remaining ones. I felt bad for their suffering.

I remember feeling instinctively happy when I saw affection, empathy, and good care of animals. One spring, we were cleaning ditches with a crew when Bucket Madsen put his arm around his old, shaggy dog and exclaimed, "This may not be the smartest dog in the world, but he sure is the ugliest." Dad was a big man, and one day when he was riding Old Blaze, a neighbor hollered, "Boots, you should get off and carry the horse for a while." In more recent years in my Wisconsin travels, I have occasionally stopped at the Hoard's Dairyman museum in Fort Atkinson and been pleased by the affection and good counsel Mr. Hoard had for the care and keeping of cows.

As I grew older, my philosophy and feelings continued to develop with many stories and truths taught about the animal kingdom. On the occasion of the march of Zion's Camp, the men found two prairie rattlesnakes one evening and were about to kill them. The Prophet Joseph instructed them to carry the snakes across the river and not harm them. He then taught them, "Let them alone—don't hurt them. How will the serpent ever lose his venom, while the servants of God possess the same disposition, and continue to make war upon it? Men must become harmless, before the brute creation; and when men lose their vicious dispositions and cease to destroy the animal race, the lion and the lamb can dwell together, and the sucking child can play with the serpent in safety."[50] The imagery of the lion and the lamb dwelling peaceably together has become sweet to me. I was pleased when my publisher chose to portray the painting of the lamb and lion at peace in Nancy Glazier-Koehler's painting *Without Any Ire* for the cover of my book *Unlocking Isaiah.* In my teaching, I have often cited the doctrine of happiness of animals as taught by John the Revelator in speaking of "four beasts"[51] and interpreted as "describing heaven, the paradise of God, the happiness of man, and of beasts."[52]

Two animal stories—one about a mama skunk and the other about a bewildered sparrow—have been real clinchers in the evolution of my current philosophy. Dad's brother, Uncle Linden, was an artist and spent his leisure time at his cabin in the mountains painting beautiful landscapes. One day he told us a story of an experience he had while irrigating our farm at the time when Grandpa Christensen still owned it. Linden had turned the irrigation water into a ditch and was keeping watch as it flowed to his desired destination. Of a sudden, he saw a mama skunk holding a baby kit in its mouth emerging from the water that was apparently flooding her den in the ditch bank. She deposited the kit safely on higher ground, then jumped back into the water and disappeared into the burrow, soon to emerge with a second kit that she placed next to the first. The mama quickly repeated the process two more times until she had her four little kits all safe. With that, she gave a scolding look at Linden and then wandered away with the kits following. Linden was overcome with emotion and reverence for the supreme love and bravery of this valiant mama who risked her life to save her kits. He told us that he decided then that he had no more interest in taking life—he would live and let live.

Some years ago, I worked at the Church Office Building for several months. I met a man, Ronald John, who became a very close friend. In his office hung a small painting of a common sparrow—so common that I paid no mind to it. Then one day Ron noticed it caught my eye and told me the story of this sparrow that his friend had painted for him. Ron had been a manager of a group of employees who had responsibility, among other things, for the care and tuning of the great pipe organ at the Tabernacle at Temple Square. One warm summer evening there had been a concert held in the Tabernacle and they had opened the doors for a while to cool the organ so it could be tuned for a repeat concert the next evening. While the doors were open, a sparrow had flown in and was not discovered until the next morning. Although this little guest had spent the night, it was not welcome to stay for the concert that evening. When Ron arrived at the Tabernacle, the crew had been trying for several hours to catch the little bird. Finally, they called animal control. They ran up and down the aisles with long-handled nets, but the bird just became more frightened. Finally in desperation, they offered to use pellet guns to dispense of the pest. Ron did not feel it would be proper to shoot holes in the ceiling of the historic Tabernacle. But he also had a reverence for life and did not want to cause any harm to the little bird. He recalled a talk by President Spencer W. Kimball teaching not to shoot the little birds.

Finally, Ron found some seclusion from the others and offered a simple prayer, "Heavenly Father, if this sparrow is important to you, could you please let us know how to safely remove it?"[53] He received a simple inspiration and instructed the workers to turn off all lights in the building and close all doors except one. As soon as this was accomplished, the little sparrow left its perch on the organ and swooped gracefully out of the open door to light and freedom.

I was very touched by Ron's story, and when he told it to me, I remembered my Christmas lines about sheaves to feed the little birds. Now at my home in Wisconsin as I write these words, I look out the window to the snow-covered bird feeder hanging just a few feet away and I see several little sparrows seeking sustenance. I delight in feeding them and I hope they will be warm tonight.

Chapter Twenty-Five:
Designated Driver

When I was about age ten or so, Dad asked if I would promise that I would never smoke cigarettes or drink alcohol. I promised him that I would not and I have kept that promise. Had he added, "smoke pot, snort cocaine, or eat Fruit Loops" I would not, at that time, have known what he was talking about. I will not attempt to recount the many benefits I have received in my life from keeping this promise, but will share one thing that has blessed me and others: I became a designated driver.

I have always loved driving. Before my retirement, I drove an average of thirty thousand miles per year for work. I have much enjoyed listening to audio books while traversing the highways and byways of Wisconsin and Upper Michigan. My car is my sanctuary—I can mostly tune out the world and enjoy my own quiet or learning time. There are, of course, some hazards to this—some years ago, my wife and I were driving to a conference in Kansas City. She was busy with a sewing project and I had my headphones on and was engrossed in a great book. I had just canceled the cruise control and checked back into reality just as I passed a state trooper. He pulled me over and said, "I could not believe you passed me when I was going the speed limit." I replied, "You know, officer, that is an amazing coincidence. I was just thinking the same thing." It cost me seventy-five dollars.[54]

I began my driving career sitting on Dad's lap on the tractor seat of our old 8N Ford as he would let me steer and run the throttle up and down. When I could reach the brakes and the clutch, I began soloing. For years on our Sunday morning paper route through Milburn, I was the designated driver—not that Dad needed one, but he wanted me to improve my driving skills. On a couple occasions, my friend Ken sneaked his mother's car while she was away and took me with him to the Fairview Cemetery to drive up and down the roads. Our rationale was that we could not hurt anyone there and few people ventured there at night.

Ron appointed me his designated driver—and he did need one on occasion. I drove us to the mountain lakes where we fished and camped. I also worked with him on his home remodeling to earn the use of his classier car for my dates and activities. I loved riding with him in the state trucks as he plowed the snow—and, to his credit, he did not allow me to drive these trucks, nor did he ever need a designated driver while on duty.

I seemed to never tire of tractor work in the fields, even after driving all day and night mowing or baling hay. I loved the times when Uncle Keith entrusted me with a load of lumber to deliver or logs or coal to haul from the mountains.

"Dragging main" was a ritual pastime in our small towns—young people drove up and down and all around in their cars with no real destination just cruising and sometimes stopping to chat or team up with others. I recall on one of my first dates, I had Ron's car and it did not occur to me that I should perhaps call home to check in about arriving late. After I dropped my date off, I teamed up with some friends for a few hours of cruising. I was embarrassed when I realized that Dad and Ron were out looking for me. I felt really grown-up and important when we drove our dates to Provo or Salt Lake for movies or concerts. Sometimes my friends did stupid things, like letting a bit of air out of their tires so they could ride the train rails. And of course there were some who raced their cars down lonely roads—I never had this problem, as my old car was not one of great power.

Big rig trucks were my real fascination. This fascination probably had beginnings when Woody Cox left his truck loaded with our lumber at our building site for a few days. It was probably a blessing that he did not leave the keys. I spent a lot of time sitting in it imagining myself traveling down the open highways. Once when I was a little older, I went with Ron in a big tanker truck to deliver oil to southern Utah. This was not a state truck—Ron was moonlighting a bit for a local supplier. He explained and demonstrated to me how to drive and then pulled over and put me behind the wheel. What a thrill! I was actually driving this huge big rig truck by myself. I did so well that after a while, Ron decided to crawl up in the sleeper for a nap. I felt so cool. That is, until I panicked and missed the gears at the bottom of a hill. Ron quickly tumbled out of the sleeper and rescued me. We experienced the mutual realization that I probably still had much to learn.

My brother Charlie was a trucker. After high school graduation, he began delivering for Granite Furniture in Salt Lake. Then, after a stint in the army and his marriage, he lived in Bakersfield and drove oil and gas tankers for his father-in-law. I was delighted when they got a contract to deliver coal spray to the mines in Castle Gate. Every few weeks, he would pull his big truck into the space between our home and the Wagon Wheel—usually in the middle of the night—and the next day, I would be able to ride with him to make the delivery in Castle Gate.

When I reached driving age, I rode with Charlie on a round trip to California and he let me drive for a long stretch through the Nevada desert. I was so excited and I determined that I might want to be a trucker someday. On another occasion after I had married, I went with Charlie to Twin Falls to deliver a load of aviation fuel and he let me drive back across the desert (Deserts seemed like the best places for me to learn). By this time, he had moved to Bountiful and he and his partners were operating their own truck line with dozens of tanker trucks on the road (Their philosophy was that they "would haul anything that they did not have to lift, shovel, carry, or poke with a stick to get on or off the truck." In other words, mostly oil and gas).

When I was a senior in high school, I met Kim Aagard of Moroni when I dated his sister-in-law. He had his own semi-truck and worked for the turkey hatchery where his father-in-law was the manager. I arranged for a week of vocational training and went with him.[55] We drove a load of grain to Los Angeles and then looped through a few stops in northern California to pick up turkey eggs for the hatchery. We stayed one night with Charlie and Betty, who still lived in Bakersfield at the time. On the return to Moroni, Kim let me drive—again across the Nevada desert.

That is the extent of my big rig driving experience. My few times behind the wheel whetted my appetite and I always wanted to do more—but mission, college, family, church, profession, and business seemed to always preclude me from doing so. Now that I am retired, I must confess that I still think about it on occasion. Who knows? One of these days I may seek training and give it a go for a time to "get it out of my system," as they say.

I remember riding along with Kim on the trip to California when a thought struck me like a lightning bolt out of the blue—I would follow the example of a few of my friends and join the Army National Guard. When I got home, I did just that. I was fascinated by the trucks and equipment of our engineer company in Mt. Pleasant and although I would later be trained and assigned as a personnel specialist, I enjoyed driving anything I could get my hands on. I think First Sergeant Chesley Christensen sensed this and often sent me driving an army pickup truck or "Deuce-and-a-Half" (army lingo for a 2.5-ton cargo truck) to Provo or Salt Lake to pick up such things as food, supplies, or rifles.

I got acquainted with Tom Nunley, the motor pool sergeant, and he regularly included me when he needed an extra driver for a convoy or special errand in our exercises. One day, Tom told me to drive a big five-ton truck from Nephi to Mt. Pleasant. I protested that I had never driven one before, but he assured me that I would do fine. I somehow got the engine started and got it in gear and pulled out into the convoy line. It seemed so big and powerful, yet it seemed like it was holding back on me or something. I thought perhaps it just did not like me and so I just kept the pedal to the floor. After I had driven a few blocks, other drivers were honking and motioning for me to stop. Smoke was pouring out the back of the truck. When Tom caught up with me, he explained this one lever that I had not seen—the emergency brake. I was so embarrassed and knew that I had likely lost my driving privilege, but this was the army, and there was money to fix my stupid errors. Tom repaired the brakes and, surprisingly, continued to let me drive. When a convoy would pull out, Tom generally stood on the side of the road to inspect the passing trucks. From that time forward, whenever I passed him, he stood with a big grin on his face and motioned to release the emergency brake. I learned my lesson.

One of my tasks in our military annual training was to sell the beer at the PX we had organized in the headquarters tent (I guess they knew that with me, it would not be a fox-guarding-the-henhouse scenario). I was rather fascinated by who drank the beer—and other products of their own procurement—and how much they consumed. One year fate aligned as I observed a couple of guys getting an early start on their booze on a Friday afternoon. The three of us were to drive home from our training site east of Salt Lake back to Sanpete for the weekend. I, of course, was the designated driver of the army issue pickup truck. After riding for an hour or so, my passengers had both fallen sound asleep with chins on their chests.

As we approached the Thistle junction (pre-mudslide), we came upon a semi-truck/tractor being towed *backwards* by a large commercial wrecker. The wheels in my brain immediately began to spin. I eased up as close to the wrecker/tractor as I felt was safe. When I sensed that the moment was just right, I simultaneously screamed, honked the horn, and tapped the brake just enough to give us a good jolt. My two passengers awoke with a start and their lives undoubtedly flashed before them when they saw nothing but a huge semi-truck coming right at them, just yards away.

I laughed as they cursed. I was grateful that there were no heart attacks. I was also grateful that all my years of designated driving had finally paid me a tremendous dividend—one of the finest moments of my life and heritage as a prankster. I knew that wherever I went and whatever I did, it could not get much better than this.

Chapter Twenty-Six:
The Future Farmer

Fred Gardner lived across the street east of Grandma and Grandpa Tucker. He was a good old guy who played the washboard in the harmonica band. I am not sure what his life profession was (he was retired when I knew him), but he seemed to tinker with farming and raising sheep. One year when I was fourteen or so, he and Dad proposed a sheep enterprise to me. Fred and I would purchase sixty old ewes that were available for nine dollars a head. They were definitely on their last lamb-bearing cycle, and we would see if we could produce one more crop. I accepted the deal and invested pretty much my life savings from my paper route and leather craft earnings. We received the ewes and randomly ran them through a dodge gate we had at our farm—each of us taking every other sheep to ensure fairness.

Fred had a great season. With several sets of twins, he got well over one-hundred percent lambing from his ewes. I got less than twenty percent lambing from my flock. I was never quite sure how this happened but suspected some moldy hay at a critical time caused them to abort early. I lost my investment, sold my ewes for pennies on the dollar, and tried to console myself that perhaps I would do better on the next venture. I learned the hard way to appreciate the risks and challenges made by farmers and ranchers. I was not sure I ever wanted to be one, but I seemed to be walking this path.

I always thought our little farm was a "for-profit" venture, but I am no longer sure. We always hoped it would be. As I reflect, I think Dad was mostly raising boys. I recall when he was once asked what he would do if he inherited a million dollars. He replied, "Oh, I would just keep on farming for a few years until it was gone." Were we farmers? Perhaps we were if we define the term "farmer" rather loosely. Our farm enterprises did not fully support our family. I just know that we worked hard on our ventures and tried several things. We raised sheep. We raised pigs mostly for our own use. For a few years, we tried Hereford cattle—Dad described their eating habits as if they had two huge scoop shovels for jaws. For several years, we raised calves that got their milk straight from the cow. This cut out the middle men so we would not have to milk them. We fed a lot of deer from our alfalfa fields—more than thirty at one counting on a summer evening. Misfortune often seemed to be our fortune.

Dad was diligent in trying to awaken me to the tasks. One cool summer morning, he got me out of bed and at least had me standing on my own by the time we got to the San Pitch property to change the water. Once he had placed the large canvas dam and the water pool had formed, he quietly reached down without warning and took hold of the cuffs of my pants with one hand and placed the other hand on the back of my neck and threw me out into the pool. I came up sputtering and coughing, but very much awake.

I worked with the spring ditch cleaning crew and especially liked playing with fire as we burned the dry grass. We cut cedar posts and built fences. I loved the smells and sights of the old Fairview roller mill when we went there for grain or farm supplies.

We did our best at doctoring. When calves got the scours (diarrhea), we had a home brew concoction that we mixed and administered with a pop bottle. Straddling the calf and holding its neck between our knees, we pulled its head upward and crammed the bottle down its throat until it consumed the mix. I soon became proficient at this task and the job was mine. We dehorned the calves and sprinkled powdered medicine on the wounds. We had a little hand-gripped device that we used to install heavy rubber bands on the lamb's testicles and tails. I made a game of chasing down the lambs and yanking their tails off at about the time they were ready to fall off anyway due to our procedure. I was alone once when I came upon a bloated sheep belonging to Big George. I had heard that a strategic knife cut could be made to relieve the bloat and save the sheep. Although I had never tried it or seen it done, I made a cut, but the sheep died. When George discovered it and knew that I had been there, he thought I had shot it. I tried to assure him that I was just a first responder trying to save his critter, but I am not sure he ever believed me.

We did our best to properly nourish and care for our livestock. Later in high school, I was awarded an agriculture scholarship to Snow College and assumed I had to spend it by enrolling in ag classes. At Snow, I signed up for a Feeds and Feeding class with my new friend Tom. The instructor began talking about all kinds of fancy formulas for feeding in varying circumstances and I was totally lost and bewildered, and I began to gain insight as to why my lambs had died from my enterprise with old Fred. Tom was already a successful rancher and went on to actually replace the professor for a time before he moved back to his ranch in Upton to become a world-renowned sheep and goat rancher. I went on to become a little-known teacher, carpet layer, and author.

Dad and I became pioneers of one of the first gravity flow sprinkler systems in the state on our "cedars" property (The "cedars" was our nickname for our sixty-plus acres just off the highway at the mouth of the canyon, and the "San Pitch" property was our fourteen-plus acres just northwest of town near the San Pitch River). The regional and state farm agents made quite a fuss over our efforts. The cedars property was hill country and had been irrigated for generations by a series of tenuous ditches that might just wash away at any moment. We hired a bulldozer to construct a holding pond at the top side of the property that would collect the water from our weekly irrigation turn. We then poured concrete to form a large box to supply the underground pipe we would install (The concrete box is still there, but the pond has been leveled). The water would flow through a pipe from the pond to the box and would then enter the down-sloping mainline pipe, which would extend the full length of the property. It was so exciting when we turned the water into the box and the mainline pipe. The air would be forced back to the top of the hill and create a roaring, raging cauldron inside the concrete box.

We contracted a backhoe to dig the long trench into which we laid the steel pipe. We hired a welder to cut a hole and install a riser every sixty feet. To irrigate, we laid aluminum sprinkler pipe across the surface of the field and connected it to the mainline with a special valve we could open and close to control the flow.

Dad, of course, had a prank for almost everything. He loved demonstrating our system to any group he could find—boy scouts, high priests, Relief Society sisters, or tourists from the Wagon Wheel (many groups used our property for socials, including the old coal stove in the cook shack we had built). He would gather them around one of the risers and leave it open at a carefully calculated degree. Then he would invite the guests to come in real close and even put their ears down near the riser so they could better hear the gurgling water and hissing air that would come shortly after he had signaled me to open the valve and turn the water into the system. As they did this, he would move casually away from the center to safe distance and then, WHOSH! When the water reached the open riser, it would spray in huge diameter, soaking all as they scrambled for safety.

As we prepared to irrigate with our new system, we had the bright idea that when we had to move the aluminum sprinkler pipes from one field to another, we would use a horse-drawn wagon rather than our tractor in order to lessen the damage to the crops. We constructed a long pipe wagon with a single tree to which we could hitch our big palomino horse Candy. We drove the wagon all around for a day or so to help Candy get used to the idea. We then ventured to move our first load of pipes to another field. We pulled Candy alongside of the line and loaded the first few pipes. As we moved to the second loading spot, one of the rubber tires of the wagon bounced over a rock that was partially buried in the ground and hidden from view by the alfalfa. As the wheel bounced, the pipes already on the wagon made a horrible, echoing, clanging noise. With that, Candy bolted for safety. Dad, of course, later described the scene with his vintage phrase, "That's when all hell broke loose!" Down the hill Candy went, headed for the corral. The faster she ran, the more ferocious her trailing monster became. Finally, when she made a sharp turn between a post and a cedar tree, the hitch broke loose and set her free from her pursuer.

We gathered up the wagon, hauled it to town, straightened it out, and installed a new hitch for the tractor, which we used from that time forward. We eventually caught up with Candy and after a good rest and some home-administered horse psychotherapy, she partially recovered—but she was always nervous from that day forward whenever we tried to hook her up to anything. We understood and tried to be gentle with her.

We once decided to grow some fancy sheep—purebred Columbias, I believe. After considerable effort and expense, we had thirty lambs ready for market and were looking forward to some reward for our efforts. One night at the San Pitch property, a pack of local dogs attacked our lambs and killed or injured half of them. We were heartsick and Dad was furious (And I have to admit that at my young age, I was more excited about the drama of it all than I was angry). The next night, Dad and I slept out in our sheep camp near the lambs. Sure enough, the dogs returned. I was sound asleep and did not know anything was happening until I heard gunshots. As I tumbled out of bed, I learned that Dad had killed one dog and wounded another. In his anger, he swore that the dog owners would pay for our ruined investment. We called the sheriff and tracked the wounded dog to its home and identified its owner—a poor widow who was saddened at the tragedy and had no means to pay. The sheriff disposed of the wounded dog and continued to investigate the case.

I was quite young and don't recall all the details, but I recall being at the house of the widow with my father. We had known her all our lives. The sheriff was there. And then we just walked away and went on about our business. I do not know the identity of the other dog owners. I suppose Dad worked that out with the sheriff in my absence. I don't remember Dad being angry anymore—as far as I knew, the case was closed, and there wasn't any grousing about our lost investment.

Just a few years before Dad died, as I was writing my personal history, I called him to get a recounting of the event. Although I knew the answer would be no, I asked him if we had ever gotten any settlement from the lost lambs. He replied, "When I realized that the dog was owned by a struggling widow, I just could not press the matter further."

From my involvement in two failed sheep enterprises, I learned sometimes we just have to cut our losses and walk away. We have to forgive. As I have experienced bigger life losses, I have remembered how Dad just walked away and tried to make the best of whatever came next. Perhaps our little farming operation was "for-profit" after all.

Chapter Twenty-Seven:

The Intersection of Haight, Ashbury, and Kirby's Lane

Occasionally I am asked if I served a foreign mission. I always reply, "Yes, in Southern California." It was certainly foreign to me—sights and sounds and cultures I had never even dreamed of. Plus, I began my mission in 1970 just in time to experience what may best be termed as the *aftershock* phase of the hippie counterculture that had so pervaded the world, the United States, and more particularly, California.

The hippie crusade of the 1960s was inspired by a generation of young people who were intent on making a statement to the world, as if to say, "We will not follow the mores of the older generation—we want our own identity." The origin of their nickname "hippie" came from the word *hip*, as in "sophisticated" or "up to date." Their mottos were such as, "Make love, not war," "Turn on, tune in, and drop out," and "Nothing is worth dying for." Their symbols included the peace sign and the placard. They dressed in tie-dyed shirts and dresses and ragged blue jeans or bib overalls with groovy patches sewn on. Their hair was long. For transportation, they drove cars or buses—a favorite was the VW bug or bus, hand-painted in their trademark psychedelic colors and displaying their mottos and lyrics. For those without a car or bus, an extended thumb became their vehicle to signal a roadside pickup, preferably by someone with an aforementioned hip bus or car.

Where were they going? They were off to Greenwich Village in New York or to the Haight-Ashbury district of San Francisco, where 100,000 of them congregated for the "Summer of Love" in 1967. In August 1969, they found their way to the Woodstock Festival in Bethel, New York. Musical accompaniment for their travels was provided by such groups as the Grateful Dead; Jefferson Airplane; The Beatles; The Rolling Stones; or Crosby, Stills, Nash and Young. John Phillips of the Mamas and Papas asked them, "Are you going to San Francisco?" and reminded them, "Put a flower in your hair."

What did they eat? They preferred what I suppose one would find at Whole Foods Markets today—fresh and organic. Perhaps this preference was a subconscious effort to counter the ill effects of the cannabis, hallucinogenic mushrooms, and LSD they ingested. What did they do? They sang, they loved, they danced, they played their guitars and they wandered the pathways of Golden Gate Park. They protested the Vietnam War and congregated to shout out their slogans to detested politicians. Occasionally a few of them laid aside their love and peace and burned or bombed something, as some did just across the way from my former institute office on the university campus in Madison, Wisconsin. A young research scientist who was a father of three children was killed. Sometimes the establishment folks got frustrated and shot back, as when National Guard troops at Kent State University in Ohio opened fire into a protesting crowd, killing four and wounding nine.

What is my assessment and opinion of the whole affair? We had this hearty generation of folks who lived through the Great Depression wearing ragged overalls and bare feet as they painstakingly worked the fields and shops in order to survive. They went off to fight in World War II, sacrificing their resources and even their lives to make a better world for their children. Then they came home to their reward of political peace and stability and economic boom and prosperity.

Some folks determined to give their children all that they themselves had been cheated of. "No child of mine will have to go barefoot or wear ragged clothes!" Perhaps they went to the extreme and should have let the children experience some of their own struggle and deprivation. Whatever the cause and the case, several of the rising generation rebelled and threw back in the faces of their parents the very things the parents so abhorred—bare feet, ragged overalls, and a listless and seemingly aimless lifestyle.

I did not go to San Francisco, nor did I put a flower in my hair (Years later, I took my daughter there out of historical interest. We wandered a few of the vintage shops where I bought her a tie-dyed shirt and we actually stood at the intersection of Haight and Ashbury, just so we could say we had been there). I listened to the music, but most of the meaning was lost on me, except when one of my more "hip" friends explained it. The only mushrooms I ate were on my salad. I did wear frayed blue jeans, but they were frayed from work in the timber or the hayfields. I was mostly neutral and uninformed about why we were in Vietnam, but I was patriotic and was preparing to serve my country as

I could. I painted my car, but in a solid color—Acapulco Blue. I did not see many hippies except on TV.

I worked for Kirby on his dairy farm where I hauled grain, mowed hay, hauled hay, cleaned stalls, hauled manure, and fed and milked the cows. Kirby's dairy barn was in town behind his home, accessible by a dirt lane running parallel to the railroad tracks. He stored farm equipment and implements along the sides of the lane. He had hired a plain-spoken and amusing old retired guy named Hilden to putter around and do what he could.

One day, I had been mowing hay when the mower broke down. I had it parked along the lane and was working on the repair when I saw a college-age couple walking toward me up the lane. I do not pass judgment. They kind of looked like hippies, both with long hair and wearing worn bib overalls. They stopped to chat with me and I learned that the boy was Kirby's nephew and he and his girlfriend were visiting from California. They were polite and pleasant and we had a good conversation.

After we chatted for a few minutes, I saw Hilden approaching from the other end of the lane. When he got to us, he looked at the two visitors and inquired, "Who are these two young ladies?" I was so embarrassed and frustrated with Hilden. Was he so old that he did not recognize who we were talking with? I replied with emphasis, "This is Kirby's *nephew* and his girlfriend." I was confident that my introduction would rescue us from a tense moment. But then I realized from Hilden's next comment that he was acting deliberately and was not at all tense about the matter. He said, "Nephew! Oh my hell, I thought you were just a big homely woman." So much for tact and diplomacy.

I do not remember what happened next—I suppose we uncomfortably ended the conversation and moved on about our tasks. But as I consider the matter now, I am fairly confident that Hilden had acted in fiduciary for his generation—boldly and straightforwardly proclaiming their bias and estimation of the whole hippie counterculture movement, even if his hearers were not what he may have supposed them to be. In any event, he seemed to have made it clear that the greatest generation would continue to live life on their own terms. Perhaps he thought, "These young folks are not as wise and sophisticated as they think they are." Or perhaps he was just being clever.

Around the time of our encounter with these California folks, Dad woke me about four o'clock one cold and rainy June morning and informed me that Kirby's dairy barn had burned down in the night. I was heartsick—not only for Kirby's loss, but with wondering if I had caused it. I had milked the cows the night before and I assumed had been the last person out of the barn. But it happened that Kirby had been out irrigating and had come through the barn after I left and he had stoked the little coal burning stove to warm up. The portion of the stove pipe that went through the attic had rusted out and apparently started the fire. In any event, the loss was total.

As soon as I got the news, I dressed and went to work. We had a hectic day of trying to figure out how to milk a herd of cows with no milking facility. Thanks to the goodness of Ron Shelley, a dairyman in Mountainville, Kirby was able to move his cows to Ron's barn, integrate them into his schedule and milk them there while he rebuilt in a new location on his land east of Fairview. I spent most of the morning on horseback, driving the cows to Mountainville. The rain continued for a while but soon cleared. I remember kind-hearted Kirby delivering a couple of lunch sandwiches to me that I ate while riding the horse.

About mid-afternoon, when things had settled a bit, a group of neighbors were standing around in Kirby's lane at the site of the fire offering their analysis. I believe Hilden was with them. I stopped in to listen. Randy Cox, then about twelve years old, was there. The men were pooling their wisdom and stating the obvious, making comments such as: "Kirby should have inspected that stove pipe," and "Perhaps the fire department should have an occasional drill so they can respond quicker when we need them." After listening to such conversation for a while, Randy spoke up and said, "You know, we should have held this meeting yesterday!"

Through my years of teaching, I have told the story of the dairy barn fire and have quoted Randy countless times in an effort to teach forethought and preparedness. If Hilden and his generation really did think that the growing generation had no wisdom, they were obviously wrong.

Epilogue:

Up, Up, and Away!

In mid-August 1969, as the hippies were headed for Woodstock, I was seventeen years old and bound for Army Basic Combat Training (BCT) and Advanced Individual Training (AIT) in Fort Leonard Wood, Missouri. As I was underage, I needed parental consent and signature to enlist. They gave it on condition that I would be given a leave of absence for two years to serve a mission, which I was granted a year later. The Selective Service Act (the draft) was in active mode and the war in Vietnam was raging. However, there was a lottery system in place to select the draftees, and my number was high, so there was little chance I would have been drafted. I enlisted from a sense of patriotism, because my friends were doing it, and because I thought it would be a good experience of new adventures and opportunities sweetened by some financial assistance to help me through college. I was not disappointed and have never regretted my decision—well, perhaps a few times during the rigors of boot camp.

I had worked the summer in the timber and in the sawmill and was in decent physical shape but was very nervous about what was ahead. As I've established, I was very sheltered from the "real world"—whatever that was. I had heard about it and was anxious.

The night before my departure, my cousin Wen let me and a friend use his auto garage to paint my old Ford car. Dad was to take the car home and store it in our garage until my return.[56] Mom fixed an early birthday/going-away dinner for me that evening, and then very early the next morning Mom and Dad drove me to the Salt Lake airport and said goodbye. I teamed up with about a dozen more recruits from Utah and reported to our escort officer, whose duty it was to deliver us to the reception center in Fort Leonard Wood.

This was my first ever plane ride (except for a quick hop from southern Idaho to Salt Lake several years before in a small, single-engine craft). I should have been excited, but I did not enjoy our flights because of my apprehension. We had a bit of a layover in Denver, and when boarding time came, our escort officer was not at the gate. We went on without him and never saw him again—I have always wondered what happened to him. Upon arrival at Fort Leonard Wood, we were herded onto "cattle trucks"—that's basically what they were, minus the manure. This would become common transportation and we soon learned to moo like cows or to sing the song from the TV cattle drive show *Rawhide* as we were rolled along. "Keep movin', movin', movin', / Though they're disapprovin', / Keep them doggies movin', / Rawhide! / Don't try to understand 'em. / Just rope, throw, and brand 'em. / Rawhide!"

At the reception center, we were greeted by a bunch of tough-talking guys with a couple of stripes on their sleeves who thought they were Generals Eisenhower or Patton—but no matter, because as far as I knew, they were. They yelled at and insulted us to no end, but I soon noticed that when an officer or someone with several stripes came around, they were subdued. We were sworn in and sworn at. We went through what seemed like endless testing. We learned the art of "hurry up and then wait," and the skill of standing in long lines for everything—medical exams, clothing issue, vaccinations, haircuts, and food. I found our dash through the barbershop to be a fascinating experience. Long-haired hippies became bald recruits in a matter of seconds. We got weekly haircuts and made a bit of a game out of timing them—they ranged from ten to twenty seconds. I once ventured a request—"just trim the sides a little and leave the top long." The civilian barber laughed and replied, "Sure, pal," and proceeded to give me the standard fifteen-second bald cut for which I was charged the standard two dollars.

When we were finally released to sleep the first night, I tried to do so as quickly as possible, as I knew the days would be rigorous. I was awakened an hour or so later by a puff of cigar smoke emitted into my face from a black guy standing with his several buddies looking down at me. They were pleasant enough—just amused that someone was sleeping. It seemed completely reasonable to me. They bantered on about their exploits back home in Chicago and invited me to go there with them on leave if we ever got the chance (We did not). They made it fairly obvious that they thought I should get out more. I later learned that some of them had been given a choice between jail and army and had chosen the army (and a few eventually had the choice rescinded and went back to jail). I eventually drifted into sleep once again amidst the growing awareness that Chicago must be quite some distance from Fairview. So was this the real world that I had been hearing about? What would the coming days and weeks be like? Would I survive?

After a few days in the reception center, we were loaded back onto the cattle trucks with all of our new clothing and equipment and hauled off to our basic training areas. We had a "zero" week to settle in, learn protocol, establish discipline, and prepare for our training schedule—and of course, everything was seasoned by generous helpings of physical training. I don't think I will ever forget army drill number one, exercise six, the push-up. We learned to properly salute and correctly address commissioned officers with such retorts as "Yes, sir," and "No, sir," and "I don't know, sir" (Someone had told me that you could get away with saying almost anything if you put a "sir" on the end of it, but I soon learned this was not true). We learned that those funny-looking hats worn by our drill sergeants were called "campaign" hats and not "Smokey the Bear" hats as we had assumed. We addressed the non-commissioned officers by their titles such as, "No, drill sergeant," or "I am from Utah, first sergeant."

September 1, 1969, was my eighteenth birthday and my first official day of basic training. I did not get a cake. We began an intense schedule of weapons training, dismounted drill, physical training, endless in-field and in-barracks inspections, target detection, quick kill, close combat, individual protective measures (such as gas masks), hand grenade training, bayonet training, hand-to-hand combat, and obstacle and confidence course training. Our leaders were mostly in between tours of Vietnam and had an abundance of stories to tell us of the atrocities of war. Many had become emotionally and spiritually hardened by their experiences.

Through it all, we cleaned our weapons, scrubbed our barracks, served on the kitchen police, picked up endless cigarette butts and litter, shined our shoes, polished our brass, made sure our socks and underwear were folded and arranged to perfection, and studied for our exams.

We made our mistakes and were punished for them. One day while we were out in the field, the cooks brought the mid-morning coffee and snack—some large sheet cakes on this occasion. Our company was divided into three training groups and my group was the first called in. The cooks failed to instruct us that the sheet cakes they had set out were intended to feed all three groups. We ate them all. When our error was detected, we were lined in a long single-file and instructed to crouch down and hold our ankles with our hands. We were then ordered to "march" in this position, appropriately called the "duck walk." As we waddled up and down the trails of the training area where all could see, we had to sing over and over, "We are the ducks that ate the cake!" But our punishment was mild compared to the screaming tongue-lashing received by the sergeants and cooks when the commander arrived.

On graduation day, we donned our full dress uniforms and paraded before our commanders and the families of some of the graduates. After graduation, we out-processed, packed our bags, and boarded the cattle trucks once again for transport across the base to our AIT training. In this new phase, we continued all of our previous physical and house-keeping routines while we proceeded with specialized combat engineer training in rigging, map reading, and using engineer tools like hand saws and jack hammers. We learned to construct expedient roads with steel, interlocking panels (think Legos for big kids). We trained in the use and firing of the M60 machine gun. We learned to throw our grenades with the M79 grenade launcher and fired 3.5 rocket launchers at rusted-out tanks and trucks. We learned to build timber bridges and set hasty obstacles and field fortifications. We blew stuff up—spending all of one morning setting a myriad of explosive charges woven together with detonation cord. After lunch, we ignited it from a safe distance of a mile or so and were then given a chance to ask debriefing questions. One soldier asked, "Drill sergeant, why did we see the explosion before we heard the sound?" I was glad that it was his question and not mine.

We learned the art of camouflage of person and property. We constructed panel bridges and learned land mine warfare. We spent several days on the Big Piney River, which flows through Fort Leonard Wood, where we constructed various types of floating bridges and learned to make expedient rafts. At night, we trained in the stealthy launching of assault boats. My squad was blessed with opportunity for many extra tries because one guy kept letting go of the spring-loaded carrying handle that slammed the boat side with awful noise. When a call was made for two volunteers with experience in driving a truck and operating a backhoe, a couple of guys beat me to the draw. I got a few hours off while one pushed a wheelbarrow (the truck driver) and the other shoveled rocks into it with a scoop shovel (the backhoe operator).

The end of our training was soon in sight and I prepared to return home, enjoy Christmas, and then try to complete a semester of college before my mission. As I out-processed and packed up for home, I reminisced on the whole experience with a flood of emotion and reflection. I wondered how my buddies whom I knew I would never see again would fare in their next assignment—many of them in the jungles of Vietnam. I contemplated college with some angst but felt a new sense of self-confidence and maturity that seemed to be propelling me forward to new challenges and experiences. I was grateful for my training and have often commented to colleagues about a particularly pugnacious teen or struggling young adult that "the best thing for him would be six months of basic training—twice a year."

On my flight home, I was excited for my pending reunion with the love of my family and the laughter of my friends. Some months before, in the midst of basic training, I had wondered if this, then, was to be the end of laughter. Training to kill people was such serious business. And then came the memorable barracks inspection. First Sergeant Murray, a no-nonsense and hardened battle veteran, was the lead inspector of the day. He had the build and demeanor of an angry bulldog. We were standing at attention at the end of our bunks and were facing the aisle. Behind us, our wall lockers proudly displayed our shirts folded uniformly to perfection. Our foot lockers were open with everything in faultless array. Our blankets were properly folded, tucked around the mattresses and stretched tight so that a quarter would bounce if dropped onto them. Just moments before the inspectors entered, I had discovered a contraband candy bar stashed under my first pair of folded trousers at the bottom of my wall locker. I had instantly recognized it as a set-up— likely from one of our drill sergeants. Such games were frequently applied to test our reaction. I had quickly disposed of the candy and then worried about what would happen when the team discovered that I had foiled their scheme.

We were arranged in alphabetical order. Private Beller was on my immediate right. I nervously glimpsed out of the corner of my eye at the advancing inspectors. Soon, First Sergeant Murray was standing face to face with Private Beller. I would be next. Murray gruffly asked, "Where are you from, Beller?" Beller replied, "Chicago." There was a long pause. I, and probably all of the other members of my platoon, if we could have, would have whispered the proper response into Beller's ear, "Chicago, *First Sergeant.*" Again through my peripheral vision, I saw Murray tense and frown and lean in toward Beller's face, almost nose to nose, and yell, "Chicago *what*, Beller?"

Private Beller, trembling and shaken, timidly replied, "Illinois."

Beller lived. He was a good sport. After running laps "until the sun goes down" as Murray had ordered him to do, we all had a good laugh. I have been laughing ever since.

About the Author

Reg Christensen, and his wife, Carol, live in Waunakee, Wisconsin. They are parents of seven children and grandparents of twelve. Their family is scattered from New York to Atlanta to Illinois to Wisconsin to Utah. Reg grew up in Fairview, Utah, and lived there until his military service at age eighteen and for a few sporadic months thereafter. Reg recently retired as Church Educational System (CES) coordinator in Wisconsin and upper Michigan and as director of the Institute of Religion adjacent to the University of Wisconsin in Madison. He began his CES career in Lehi, Utah, where he taught released-time seminary for twenty-three years. Through the years of his profession, he and his family also operated a floor-covering sales and installation business. Reg has had varied church callings, including branch president, bishop, and stake executive secretary. He currently serves as his ward early morning seminary teacher and teaches an adult religion class on Isaiah. He and his wife also currently serve as missionaries for the BYU Idaho Pathway program. Reg enjoys reading, traveling, exploring nature, doing handyman projects, bird watching, and being with family and friends. In his spare time, he also writes books—this one is number five.

Books by Reg Christensen

Fear Not: Messages of Hope, Healing, and Peace in the Book of Revelation (2010)

Worthy is the Lamb: Scriptural Insights of Peace and Joy from Handel's Messiah (2012)

Joyful Apocalypse: Unveiling the Messages of Joy and Hope in the Book of Revelation (2013)

Unlocking Isaiah: Lessons and Insights that Draw Us to the Savior (2013)

Regular: The Saga of a Regular Guy from an Extraordinary Place (2014)

Endnotes

(* = Author's Note)

---

1 William Jenson Adams, *Sanpete Tales: Humorous Folklore from Central Utah*, (Salt Lake City: Signature Books, 1999).

2 *This new home built by my Christensen grandparents (on the west side of 200 East, half way between 200 and 300 North) was just a block and a half to the north of the home of my Tucker grandparents. The home still stands today, but I do not know who lives there.

3 Helaman 5:12.

4 *A more modern beekeeper would likely not recommend any kind of manure in a smoker. One guy explained that manure contains E. coli bacteria that can be transferred to honeycomb and from there to the honey gathering equipment and from there to—well, you get the picture, I am sure. A friend of mine—one of the top beekeepers in Wisconsin—confirmed this information.

5 *The old rock Larsen home, at the time of this writing, still stands on the southwest corner of State and Center Streets.

6 *This is currently the site of Walker's Food and Fuel.

7 *Grandma Turpin lived in a brick home on the north side of 200 South, between State Street and 100 West.

8 3 Nephi 8:18.

9 *I feel a need to confess that I have been a bit embarrassed in recent decades to refer to the San Pitch as a "river." I have thought that perhaps "stream" or "creek" might be better terms. My problem was that I had been comparing it to some of the major rivers near my current home— the Fox, the Rock, the Wisconsin, and the Mississippi. But I have now reconciled this dissonance. I grew up with the "San Pitch River," so "river" it is!

¹⁰ *I have restricted this sampling of names mostly to folks who lived in Fairview and were within a few years of my own age. If I were to list the many other wonderful friends I had/have who are older and younger and from other communities, the listing would be huge.

¹¹ *I think I may have even asked the pilot if he would take us for a ride and let me sit by him in the cockpit—but to no avail. I still attempt this ploy today with my son who is a commercial airline pilot—but still to no avail. The other day, I even tried this with my son's friend who was piloting us from Salt Lake to Madison, but he did not fall for it either. But my son tells me that this could yet happen if we can find a time when he has to fly an empty plane to a distant city for painting or mechanical work (I think I will have him get the work done first and then just fly the return with him).

¹² *Just in case someone needs an explanation, a modern grain "combine" is named such because it combines the cutting, threshing, and winnowing of wheat or other grain into one process with one machine. Our binder would cut the wheat, without threshing, and bind it into bundles to be hauled to the threshing site. At that point, the bundles would be fed into the threshing machine to separate the wheat from the straw or chaff.

¹³ *In referencing *Dennis the Menace*, I am referring to the live-actor TV series that ran from 1959 to 1963 and not the comic strip of the same name that inspired the TV series and was written by Hank Ketcham.

¹⁴ *The idea for this chapter came from an introduction my friend Ed Cox gave of me when I spoke in a meeting he had invited me to. He said something like, "I don't think Reg ever did anything wrong in our growing up years." I considered that, as part of my penance, I should try to set the record straight.

¹⁵ *I share this account with permission from Louise Christensen, my sister-in-law.

¹⁶ *I struggled as to whether or not to even include my memories of the old minstrel shows. I decided to share not to emphasize or glorify in any way the concept of a minstrel show performance, but rather to portray an important time of my life with my father. I am fully aware that these shows were perceived by some to denigrate the culture and heritage of African Americans. However, I do not defend or assault the producers and performers of the Fairview shows—they were who they were and they acted with the limited knowledge they had at the time. Personally, I do not think they were racist. I just think they were caught up in a popular fad of the day. I will leave their judgment to God. I believe

that they felt they were doing good to provide entertainment and to fundraise for a worthy cause. I would hope and do believe that had we had an African American population in Fairview during this time, they would have been welcome to eat at the lunch counters just like everyone else and that Dad would have been there visiting and eating with them and enjoying their company.

17   *My wife and I visited Grandpa Tucker a just few years before he died at age 95 and had him strum his guitar and sing some of his old songs, including a rendition from the old shows.

18   Doctrine and Covenants 130:2.

19   Dorothy Stowe, "Feel America's Pulse at Folksy Little Museum," *Deseret News,* July 28, 1978.

20   Lee Benson, "About Utah: Longest Marriage? Utahn Says Otherwise," *Deseret News,* June 17, 2005.

21   Ibid.

22   Ed Cox, "You Can Do Hard Things," *Snow College-Richfield Campus Commencement Address,* Friday, May 3, 2013.

23   Ibid.

24   Alma 30:15.

25   Articles of Faith 1:13.

26   Alma 17:2.

27   *This quote is apocryphal. The man who told it to me said that President Young was supposedly once handed a diary by a young girl requesting his autograph. He accepted her request and wrote this couplet in her book.

28   Kai Bird & Martin Sherwin, *American Prometheus: The Triumph and Tragedy of J. Robert Oppenheimer* (New York, N.Y.: Alfred A. Knopf, 2005).

29   *President Kennedy made this declaration, sometimes known as his "Moon Shot" speech, to a joint session of Congress on May 25, 1961, my Dad's forty-eighth birthday.

30   *This training paid me a dividend years later as I was teaching seminary and a moment of decision came our way. Our fire alarm went off for a routine drill. One girl panicked and yelled out, "Oh my gosh— FIRE! Quick, everyone get under your desks!" I was able to calmly say, "No, Emily, I think that is for earthquake. I think this is a *fire* drill, so let's all go outside and away from the building."

31   *I was so impressed that I later married his granddaughter. But, in all fairness, I must add that I did not make this connection from his speech to my wife until many years after we were married when Dad reminded us of it.

[32] *Some have spoofed the event, claiming that Brother Brigham had surveyed the desolate valley and then said something like: "If ever in the wide expanse of God's earth there were a barren, useless wasteland, this is the place! Drive on to California."

[33] Isaiah 5:26.

[34] James E. Faust, "Eternity Lies before Us," *Ensign*, May 1997 (Also quoted by Heber J. Grant in *Conference Report*, April 1921, 211).

[35] *This is the current location of Dr. Steven Bench's dental office.

[36] *In the past few months, I hand-tooled a water lily for a decorative top of an heirloom trunk I made for my daughter. I also hand-tooled my most intricate design ever—a roots and branches image of a mulberry tree for a remembrance plaque of my son-in-law's parents. For both of these projects, I printed an image from the Internet, traced it onto leather, and then tooled it using my original junior high tools.

[37] *I gave one rifle case to my brother Ron and kept one for myself. Ron subsequently wore out and discarded the chaps and his rifle case. My son is keeping mine as an heirloom.

[38] *If you are in Fairview and you are interested, you might just drive up the canyon road to the canyon's mouth, turn north on this lane, and drive to the top of the hill so you will better understand what I am trying to explain here.

[39] https://www.trumanlibrary.org/lifetimes/whouse.htm

[40] *I currently live in Wisconsin and snowmobiling is quite popular. Eagle River, part of my former CES area, even boasts of being the "Snowmobile Capital of the World." But the sport is way different here—the normal activity is to cruise the marked trails through open farmer's fields with calculated stops at the neighborhood bars along the way. When folks tell their stories, I mostly just daydream about my youth, the majesty of Fairview's mountains, and the wild and crazy times we had.

[41] *A few times over the years, I have been asked to share something unique about myself in a social setting. Sometimes the group is assigned to guess who's who based on anonymous responses. I have had fun writing "I once dug a grave in the middle of the night," then observing the conjecture of the others as they try to figure it out.

[42] *Jerry went on, like Uncle Keith, to serve as mayor and bishop of Fairview. Coincidentally, I noticed on Facebook from Jerry's daughter Mary that the very day of this writing is the tenth anniversary of his death. He died doing what he loved—cutting timber up in the mountains.

43 *Some years later, after my mission, the speech team and coach of Snow College recruited me to go with them and try my hand at informative speaking. I chose the topic of "How to Fell a Tree" and presented it, complete with visual aids of saw, posters, and hard hat. For doing this, they gave me a few trophies—so I guess I got my accolade fix after all.

44 * My insights are recorded in my book *Worthy is the Lamb: Scriptural Insights of Peace and Joy from Handel's Messiah.*

45 *Just in case I have misled anyone here, President Richard Nixon made his "I am not a crook" statement five years later at a press conference on November 17, 1973, just months before he would resign as president due to the scandal sparked when members of his staff orchestrated a break-in to the Democratic National Committee headquartered in the Watergate Hotel in Washington, DC.

46 *There has been some dispute over whether he said "for a man" or "for man" but he affirms "for a man," so I take him at his word. Or perhaps he said, "That's one small step for a man; one giant leap for Tang breakfast drink," but I have my doubts about that (Tang was the official drink of the astronauts, and I am sure the moon landing was a giant leap for its producers).

47 *Since my intent is not to give a detailed and documented account of the shooting, I am just offering some general expressions that are consistent with my understanding of events, prompting my memory with an online timeline of the assassination. A man named Abraham Zapruder produced, with a home movie camera, what is likely the most complete and clear video of the shooting. After a media frenzy to obtain the film, he negotiated to sell it to *Life Magazine.* This Zapruder film was one of the main sources of examination used by the later-appointed Warren Commission.

48 2 Nephi 30:16.

49 *Here is a bit of context for this quote, taken from the Wikipedia entry for Red Ryder BB gun: "The Red Ryder BB gun was prominently featured in *A Christmas Story* in which Ralphie Parker requests one for Christmas, but is repeatedly rebuffed with the warning 'You'll shoot your eye out.' The movie's fictional BB gun, described as the 'Red Ryder carbine-action, two hundred shot Range Model air rifle with a compass in the stock and this thing which tells time,' does not correspond to any model in existence nor even a prototype; the Red Ryder featured in the movie was specially made to match author Jean Shepherd's story (which may be artistic license, but was the configuration Shepherd claimed to

remember). However, the 'Buck Jones' Daisy air rifle, immediately above the Red Ryder in the Daisy line, did have a compass and sundial in the stock, but no other features of the 'Red Ryder' model. The guns and a stand-up advertisement featuring the Red Ryder character appeared in a Higbee's store window in the film, along with dolls, a train, and Radio Flyer wagons."

50 *History of the Church*, 2:71.

51 Revelation 4:6.

52 Doctrine and Covenants 77:2.

53 Ronald D. John, "A Sparrow in the Tabernacle," *Ensign*, June 1989, 24.

54 *Several years ago, I was driving through the middle of Iowa in return from a CES conference and was so into my audio book that I realized upon pausing I was way out in the midst of a bunch of corn fields and had no clue where I was or even which direction I was traveling. I had no GPS in those days, so I had to find my way back with a map. And just two days ago, I was returning from my daughter's home in Oshkosh and was talking on the phone with her. After I hung up, I drove another twenty minutes or so before I realized I had taken a wrong turn and was somewhere I did not recognize. I was able to use my GPS this time, but it took me almost an extra hour to get home.

55 *My son is currently a young-looking commercial airline pilot. A few years ago as he greeted boarding passengers, a lady said to him, "You look like you are in high school." He laughingly replied, "I am in high school—they gave me a week off to learn to fly airplanes."

56 *On my very first day home in December, I got the car out of storage and drove it to the cedars to feed the cattle. As the snow was too deep to drive in to the barn area, I drove partway up the lane, parked, and then hiked to the barn. When I got back, the car was gone. To my dismay, I discovered that it had slid down the snow-packed hill and landed in a ditch. There was serious scratching the full length of the side of the car from the end of a steel culvert—so much for my new paint job.